MODERN HINDUISM
Insights for Non-Hindus and Hindus

What each Hindu ought to know and
What every non-Hindu should know

For Muslims, Christians and Others
Also for the Non-Believers World Over

Ashok Garde

MODERN HINDUISM:
Insights for Non-Hindus and Hindus

What each Hindu ought to know and
What every non-Hindu should know

For Muslims, Christians and Others
Also for the Non-Believers World Over

Ashok Garde

Publisher:
Continental Prakashan,
2159/2, Vijayanagar Colony, Pune 411004

Printed at
N. K. Printers, Rakhial, Ahmedabad 380023

Typesetting:
Media Creations, Bodakdev, Ahmedabad 380 059

Cover Page:
Manoj Rana, Ahmedabad

ISBN 978-81-7421-159-0

Publication Number: 1705

First Edition: 2014

(Published by Author as E-Book on Kindle,
www.amazon.com 26.06.2013)

Price: ₹ 150

Contents

Dedicated

To my father, **Dr. R. K. Garde**
for encouraging me to delve into philosophy
and
To **Dr. Govind N. Sharma,**
Calgary, Canada, for stimulating discourses
on religions

Grateful thanks

To **Mr. P.V.R.N. Iyer**
for financial support, offered spontaneously
on his own for wider dissemination of
Modern Hinduism.

Modern Hinduism
What each Hindu ought to know and
What every non-Hindu should know

Hundreds of books exist on Hinduism, but a short version
describing the way Hinduism has re-cast itself to remain
relevant in the modern world, the core concepts and the practices of
Hinduism in the 21st Century is missing. This 80-pages booklet
attempts to cover this lacuna. Its aims are:

For Hindus: to give a firm foundation in their dharma

- The great heritage of Hinduism, a living culture of over
  7000 years, is brought out. (Ch. 1)
- The rationale behind the multiplicity of religious ways of
  the Hindus is explained.(Ch. 3)
- The philosophical underpinning of Hinduism is described,
  including that of idol worship.(Ch. 5)
- The historical struggle of Hinduism to reform and to
  become a modern religion is outlined.(Ch. 4)

This knowledge will help each Hindu to explain the basis for the
diverse practices of Hinduism to others, while clearly pointing out
how the 'bad' concepts and practices have been eliminated.

For non-Hindus: to help others, especially Christians and
Muslims, to understand Hinduism

- How Hinduism exists and flourishes without a source of
  'authority' or organization. (Ch. 7)

- The rationale behind the multitude of paths and practices of this 'complex' 'religion'. (Ch. 3, 6)
- The theoretical basis for idol worship, many gods, and even animal worship. (Ch. 5)
- The role of temples in personal and social life: of gurus, pilgrimages and festivals. (Ch. 7)
- The logical basis for Hinduism not being a proselytizing religion. (Ch. 3)

This information would not only generate a sympathetic understanding of Hinduism but may also lead to a wish to adopt some views and practices of Hinduism without compromising on own religion.

For the curious non-believer: to help understand how Hinduism is also a 'no-God' religion

- How Hinduism has grown as the third most followed religion without proselytizing. (Ch. 3, 7)
- How Hinduism as a religion has never been in conflict with progress of science. (Ch. 6)
- Why atheists/ agnostics may feel attracted to some thought processes of Hinduism. (Ch.3, 6)
- How to acquire mental peace and physical fitness from some practices of Hindu origin. (Ch.7, 8)
- How Hinduism can help the world to become a multi-religion society without conflicts. (Ch. 8)

Progress of science and rational thinking has challenged the notion of 'God in the image of man'. Those who do not accept 'faith' will find the philosophies of Hinduism worthy of their attention.

The stance for the contents of this booklet is: to simplify without loss of authenticity, to include only the core concepts, and to avoid mentioning Hindu achievements in sciences, literature and arts. The philosophy, the ideas about god and liberation, and the place of individual in society under Hinduism are covered: but not the ideas on creation of the universe; the legends about gods, heaven, and hell; the subtle bodies and miraculous capabilities etc. All these are considered peripheral to the normal practice of Hinduism by the populace. Causes taken up for reforms from 1800 CE are mentioned exhaustively; but names of only some prominent reformers, out of the hundreds, are mentioned.

CHAPTER 1
Dharma: Great Heritage

Hindu, India and Hinduism were words used by people from outside India to label the people, the country and the 'religion' of the inhabitants of this sub-continent in Asia. These were accepted later by Hindus and Indians also, and are in common usage since 1800 CE. All three stem from the name of the river Sindhu (Indus in Greek), the main river of the Northwest, where 's' was pronounced like 'h' by the Persians and the Arabs. The earliest known mention of the word Hindush for India is found in Zoroastrian work of 486 BCE. By about 600 CE the word Hindu as people of India became common, and by 1100 CE, the Persians termed the country of Hindus as Hindu-staan*. The Greeks had called the country as India since about 440 BCE, but Hinduism as a word for the 'religion' was coined around 1700 CE. Since around 6000 BCE, the name of the country was Aaryavarta which expanded later into Bhaaratvarsha. The inhabitants called themselves as Aaryas* (aarya = noble person), their language was Sanskrit, and the word used for their system of conducting life was dharma. Dharma has over 16 meanings in Sanskrit: duty, characteristic property, quality, justice, holy, law, ethics, morals, etc. and also something like 'religion'.

---

* *Pronunciation of Sanskrit words: When a word occurs for the first time in this text, 'aa' is used to show that the pronunciation is long, like 'a' in 'calm'. The use of 'a' at the end of a noun/word indicates only the completion of a consonant and is to be pronounced short. Thus, Aarya is written the first time, and the commonly used spelling Arya is used thereafter.*

When the Aryans came into India from central Asia sometime during 8000 BCE and 5000 BCE[#] their 'scriptures' were the four Vedas, which gave details of their dharma. They found a flourishing original culture in India, termed the Indus valley culture (7500 to 2500 BCE) in the North with overlapping culture in the South (later termed Dravidian culture by some Indologists of 18th century CE). Each had an impact on the other. These two cultures together became a pan-Indian Hindu culture and religion that encouraged learning and questioning everything about life and its purpose. This culture continued

---

[#] *The commonly accepted period for the appearance of Vedas is around 1500 BCE. This was estimated by Frederick Maxmueller in ca 1870 CE based on changes in the Sanskrit language. Starting with a historically reliable date of Gautama Buddha (ca 600 BCE), he worked backwards in 4 steps of 200 years to determine the age of the Vedas. (Some scholars have suggested 500 years and 1000 years per step). These periods are extrapolations from similar changes in Greek and Latin over known periods. All extrapolations are of doubtful validity and need confirmation from other sources to be considered valid. B.G.Tilak, based on evidence from Rig-Veda, proposed (1903) that the Vedas were revealed in the arctic regions and the Aryans migrated into India sometime during 8000 and 5000 BCE. Archeological evidence accumulated over 1920 -1994 CE on sites at Mehrgarh, Mohen Jo Daro, Harappa and Lothal clearly shows that the Harappan civilization had continuous existence from 7000 to 2500 BCE. Use of cotton, wheat, barley, tanning, copper and bronze tools, mud huts, preliminary dentistry, brick making in kilns and planned sanitation in cities are some of the findings. The historicity of Rama of the epic Ramayana has not yet been established; but the birth date of Rama can be estimated from the position of stars as in 5315 BCE. The historicity of Mahabharata and the war at Kurukshetra is established and the period is ca 3000 BCE. The timeline used in this booklet is thus based on the findings accumulated over the years. [Claims on antiquity of Vedas going to over 10,000 years have been ignored.] Given the methods of estimation of these periods, the accuracy of each may be taken as + or – 500 years till about 1000 BCE, and about + or - 50 years till about 700 CE, when specific dates are not known. The years when visitors from the East and the West came to India have been neatly recorded by them, starting from the invasion of Alexander in 326 BCE. After Muslim invasions started in ca 700 CE, most events were accurately dated and recorded by their historians; thereafter, historical record keeping in India improved substantially.*

to adapt, survive and thrive over the next seven millennia; and is a living culture of present day India. Philosophy, religious sects, arts and sciences flourished (and waned) over this period, during which India was ruled by many dynasties. Several *gana-raajya* (republics), where rulers were selected by people, also existed around 600 BCE.

Every religion has a say on two aspects of life: the individual in relation to a superpower and the individual in society. The religion of the rulers and their policies towards religion(s) of their subjects together exert a large influence on the contents and spread of religions. So, let us review the period from 7000 BCE to 2000 CE to see what was happening on the political scene in relation to Hinduism.

Bharatvarsha of 5000 BCE consisted of part of Afghanistan besides the entire sub-continent below the Himalayas. Early (7000 BCE) Vedic kings –*raajan* –were tribal chiefs, and the later periods saw small Kingdoms with Kings administering them according to the dharma laid down by their priest-gurus. The first dynasty was Ikshwaaku, known also as the family of Raghu. The genealogy of the Ikswaku dynasty shows King Dasharatha as the 36th ruler. King Dasharatha of Ayodhyaa (5000 BCE), bound by a promise to one of his three wives, had to ask his eldest son Rama to go in exile in a forest for fourteen years, so that her son Bharata, could rule the kingdom. Rama's brother Laxmana and his wife Sitaa accompanied him to the forest Dandaka in South. There, the King Raavana of Lankaa abducted Sita in the thirteenth year, and was rescued after a war in Lanka that killed Ravana. Thereafter, Rama returned to Ayodhya and Bharata, who had ruled in Rama's name, returned the kingdom to Rama. This story of Rama–the

Raamaayana - and his benevolent rule for long years made him so famous that Rama was idolized as the best of men and became, in the course of time, a major deity for the Hindus.

The next major dynasty is of the Kurus (3000 BCE). The Great War between the 100 sons- Kauravas - of the blind King Dhrutaraashtra and their 5 cousins, the Paandavas (sons of King Pandu) is the main topic of the epic Mahaabhaarata. King Krishna of the Yadavas lent his army to the Kauravas and guided the Pandavas towards success in this war where the Pandavas were forced to fight for their due rights. A large number of small kingdoms under the protectorate of Kauravas and Pandavas are mentioned in Mahabharata. King Krishna opted to be the charioteer of Arjuna, the second of the Pandava brothers. When Arjuna hesitated to start a war on his cousins, senior relatives and even teachers, merely to enjoy a kingdom, Krishna advised him in several ways as to why he should not shirk this unpleasant task. This advice summarizes the philosophies and practices of the dharma (later called Hinduism) that is a good synthesis of the Aryan Vedic and originally Indian –Dravidian– thoughts and practices. [The epics Ramayana and Mahabharata were composed by different authors over a period of about 1000 years starting around 1000 BCE. The stories were passed on by bards singing them and were later put down in written form. When Krishna's advice was 'expanded', probably during 100 BCE to 100 CE, the philosophies expounded in the Upanishadas parts of the Vedas were incorporated as a part of the advice. More importantly, King Krishna became Lord Krishna, God manifesting in human form.] Since Lord Krishna's discourse is in verse form, it is known as Bhagavad-Geetaa (Celestial Song) and is considered as one of the main scriptures of Hinduism. God Krishna is a prominent deity of Hinduism today.

From 7000 BCE to 600 BCE, there was only one 'religion' in India: the Vedic dharma influenced by the Shiva worship of Dravidians, which the Aryans had called 'sanaatana dharma' –eternal religion. Jainism and Buddhism appeared around 700 - 600 BCE. Both Mahaavira, the main founder of Jainism and Gautama, the founder of Buddhism, were princes of small kingdoms. They gave up their kingship in favor of 'search for truth'. From 700 to 320 BCE, the Haryaanka, Shishunaaga and Nanda dynasties ruled in the North. When 'Alexander the Great' from Greece invaded India (327 BCE), he conquered several kingdoms and established Seleucus as his successor in the Eastern region of India. Samraat (emperor) Chandragupta Maurya (who ruled from 322 to 298 BCE) replaced the Nanda dynasty and built a large empire. He defeated Seleucus and Indian hegemony was re-established. The Maurya dynasty lasted for 136 years. Samrat Ashoka (269 to 231 BCE), who spread Buddhism worldwide, was from this dynasty. Later, Emperor Vikramaditya of the Parmaar dynasty who ruled from Ujjaini, started an era termed Vikram Samvat in 57 BCE. In the South, the dynasty from 230 BCE till about 200 CE was of Saatavahana, of which the Emperor Shaalivahana started a new era termed Shaka in 72 CE. Both these calendars are in use in India today, mainly in the context of religious festivals and rituals. (The official Indian calendar is Gregorian, as the common world calendar. So, all references in this book are in terms of Common Era -CE.) Without exception, rulers promoting a particular religious order – Jainism, Buddhism, Vaishnava (Krishna) or Shaiva (Shiva) sects of Hinduism – also let the other orders flourish.

In the North, the Maurya dynasty was followed by the Kushaan and the Gupta dynasties, each ruling for about three centuries. Emperors Kanishka and Emperor Samudragupta were from these two dynasties. The period from 300 to 600 CE is considered the Golden Period of Hindus, since many advances in mathematics, astronomy and science took place and the fine arts blossomed in many forms. During this period, the dynasties in the South were: Pallava, Paandya, Kadamba, Chaalukya, Cholaa. In the East were Kharavela, Verman and Paala; in the West were Kshatrapa, Vaataataka and Raashtrkuta. Most rulers were Hindu, some promoted Jainism and some Buddhism. By the time the Muslim invasions started in 711 CE, the North had fragmented into many small kingdoms. Muslim rulers started consolidating their kingdom in India from 1100 and became *Indian* rulers from 1550 in the North. During 900 to 1500, the South, the East and the West were ruled mainly by Hindu dynasties: Kalaachuri, Hoysaala, Naayaka, Vijaynagar Empire and Cholaa in the South; and Sena, Ganga, Mlencha in the East; Maitraka, Yaadava, and Pratihaara in the West. Like Buddhism earlier, Hinduism also spread eastward in Indonesia and Cambodia, where the influence of the two epics Ramayana and Mahabharata have persisted over long periods of several centuries, including the 21st century, in spite of the rise of Islam.

From 1100, the North and many more parts of India were ruled by Muslim rulers: the main dynasties ruling from Delhi were Slave, Tughlak and Lodi. The Mughal dynasty ruled from 1550 to 1760. The South had a separate Sultanate named Bahamani from 1347 till 1525, which then split into 5 Sultanates of Muslim rulers. All the Muslim rulers were guided by the Holy Quran and the Sharia laws. Several rulers tried to enforce those directives from the Holy Quran that say 'non-believers, kafirs, idol worshippers' should either be converted to Islam or may be killed. Large scale massacres by Moghul invaders were a consequence of such dictates. Some Sharia laws, such as enforcing the 'jizia' tax of about 50% on non-Muslims other than the followers of 'book religions' (Jews and Christians) were also implemented by many Islamic rulers on their Hindu/Budhists/Jain citizens who were a very large majority. Emperor Akbar the Great was the only Moghul emperor who treated Hindus fairly. The socio-political environment created by the Muslim rulers had several consequences for Hindus and for Hinduism. One major impact was the founding of Sikhism in 1500 by Guru Nanak in Punjab. Sikhism picked up the good parts of Islam and of Hinduism and spread fast, also with the support of Hindus. (The shia-sufi movement within Islam that grew over this period was essentially a bhakti – devotion –movement similar in some ways to the several bhakti sects that flourished within Hinduism. The Sufis had no conflict with idol worshipping Hindus because of their strong belief in unity of God. However, most Muslim rulers were Sunni/Shia Muslims who together formed a majority within Islam in India.)

The period after 1550 saw the rise of the Rajput,Maratha and Sikh powers in opposition to the Muslim rulers. Maharana Pratap in Rajasthan, Chatrapati Shivaji in Maharashtra and Maharaja Ranjit Singh in Punjab established kingdoms to protect Hindus and Sikhs from the bad treatment by Muslim rulers. It is important to note that the Muslim population in their kingdoms received fair treatment and several masjids were given government support also. By the middle of the 18th century, Marathas had become the most powerful and the East India Company from Great Briton had consolidated its power in the East and in the South. This British trading company, empowered by the government in Great Briton to raise and use an army in India for ensuring trading rights, had 'conquered' the entire country by 1820. The numerous small kingdoms in India became protectorates of the 'company'. A major revolt took place against the British in 1857-58. Lead primarily by the (Sunni Wahhabi) Muslim clerics and joined by Hindus and Muslims in the army, this revolt was backed by a few kingdoms and was also partly supported by the people. This 'first war of independence' was put down forcefully by the E. I. Company. This led to a takeover of India as a colony by the British Crown, whereby the Queen of Great Briton became the sovereign for India. The Portuguese and the French also had acquired small territories on the west and east costs of India. This colonization came to an end in 1947, after the Indians fought for their independence in a mostly non-violent way under Mahatma Gandhi. The nearly 250 years of British influence and about 150 years of British rule over India had tremendous impact on India, on Hindus, on Muslims, and on Hinduism.

The Muslim rule of over 900 years had been harsh on the Hindus; conversion to Islam by force and by inducement had resulted in about one fourth of India's population being Muslims as the 20th century began. Many Muslims, mostly the upper classes, were unhappy about having lost their status as rulers and were also apprehensive that a nation with majority of Hindus would not be fair to them after gaining independence from the British. Consequently, a two-nation theory was proposed by claiming that Muslims and Hindus should be two separate nations. Many Muslims who had participated in the struggle for independence did not accept the two-nation concept. However, the demand for a separate Pakistan – a nation for Muslims - in provinces of India where the Muslims were a majority was accepted by all and India was divided into two nations in 1947. In 1971, the Bengali speaking East Pakistan separated from West Pakistan and became Bangladesh. In the 21st century, Pakistan is the second most populous Muslim country in the world after Indonesia; and the population of Muslims in Pakistan, India and Bangladesh is of the same order. The bifurcation of India on the basis of religion and a large Muslim population in India have had their multifactor impact on Hindus and Hinduism.

This brief review of the socio-political scene over 7000 years shows that almost all non-Muslim rulers permitted the Vedic religion, Jainism, Buddhism, Hinduism, Islam, Sikhism and also Christianity to flourish ; no religion was ever persecuted or banned. Most Muslim rulers, guided by Quran, took many steps to convert Hindus, attacked Hindu temples to destroy idols, and in general looked at Hindus as second grade citizens with a religion of the wrong kind. They employed Hindus in many capacities, but always under a Muslim chief. The Hindus had to manage to keep their religion intact by using means like the bhakti movement that took Hindu persons from all rungs of the society into the fold of religion. During the British rule, the government kept away from the proselytizing efforts of the Christian missionaries, even when all the rulers were Christians.

We now turn to the social system of Hinduism, followed by its ideas on salvation.

CHAPTER 2
Dharma: Individual and Society

Hinduism has a comprehensive scheme for the way in which an individual should play a role which is meaningful for each and which is consistent with good sustenance of society over long periods. The three dimensional scheme developed and used over a period of nearly 7000 years is shown in Figure 2.1.

This *varna-aashrama-purushaartha* system describes the totality of life of an individual in society. The life of an individual –X axis - has been divided into four natural phases: learning,

Figure 2.1
Hindu Structure for Ethics
A three dimensional societal system

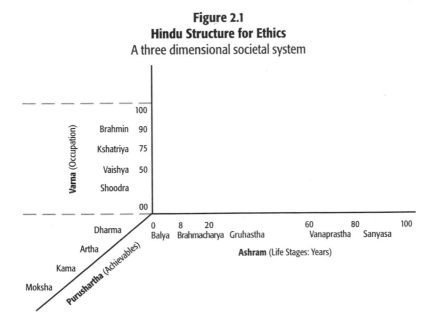

earning, detaching and exiting. These are termed as brahmacharya (spiritual conduct), gruhastha (householder), vaanaprastha (forest living) and sanyaasa (complete withdrawal). The approximate number of years in each phase in the lifespan of 100 years is shown on the X axis. Schooling was by Gurukul system, where the pupil goes to the ashram (hermitage) of a guru and lives with his family for 12 years. There he learnt about Vedas and philosophies, sciences, martial arts, dharma/morals; and learnt humility and virtuous behavior from his guru as his role model. Well equipped to take up a vocation to earn and to maintain a family, he proceeded to the next phase - householder. This phase is the most important for the well-being of the society because its twin task of wealth generation and of sustenance of the other three stages of life. After 35-45 years as householder, one has achieved whatever he could in life, and feels that his 'burden' of responsibilities may be passed on to the next generation. This starts the stage of detachment – vanaprastha - going away for a simple living in a forest. By the age of 80-90, time is ripe for a 'life after', accepting serenely the approach of death. The sanyasa phase is meant for devoting entire energies to spiritual pursuits.

The Y-axis shows the fourfold classification of occupations: the priests and the lifelong learners / teachers are Braahmins; those who protect the society maintaining law and order are Kshatriyas; those who generate wealth by way of farming, animal husbandry and trade are Vaishyas; and the rest who are craftsmen and entertainers, and who are employed for various services are the Shoodras. Their approximate proportion in society is indicated in percentages.

The Z-axis has no scale. The four purusharthas -goals or achievables of life for each individual – are not to be achieved one after another; they are to be pursued simultaneously all through one's life. Dharma stands for personal, familial, societal and religious duties; and for ethics, morals and laws. Dharma needs to be followed while pursuing the other three purusharthas –life goals. Artha stands for earning resources for the family and thereby also creating wealth for society. Kaama is the fulfillment of desires of self as well as of the family and the society. Moksha stands for liberation or for release from this world, or for unification with the supreme power. When earning and satisfying desires are seen to result in 'diminishing returns' of happiness, one wonders why, and begins to seek 'the' purpose of life. Moksha, an important and vital concept of Hinduism, pervades all activities of the life of Hindus (Chapter 3). Outside this system were few who renounced the world early in life to become sanyaasins – the category of monks or yogis.

This three dimensional framework is clearly a formalization of the natural processes that take place in any society. It also defines the Do's and Don'ts for a Hindu and may as well be considered as Hindu ethics. This framework, based on inherent qualities of persons leading to choice of profession, looks neat; but it had major lacunae that led to rather confounding consequences. Let us have a quick look at the good, bad and the ugly aspects of this three dimensional societal system.

Good: The emphasis on education and on earning for satisfying desires as a householder form parts of religious duties; this makes the religion easier to follow. The concepts of detachment and giving up worldly responsibilities also work for the good of the old and the young. Each individual knew his/her place and role in society: Brahmins were expected to be strong on spirituality and unattached to money; Kshatriyas strong on courage and on using power; Vaishyas strong on wealth generation and sharing; and Shoodras strong on delighting those whom they serve. Moral behavior for all consists of ten aspects of dharma: dhruti- fortitude, kshamaa-forgiveness, dama-control, asteya-non-stealing, shoucha-cleanliness, indriya-nigraha- control of organs, dhee-wisdom, vidyaa-knowledge, satyam-truth, akrodha-non-anger. The six enemies that need to be conquered are: kama-lust, lobha-greed, krodha-anger, mada -pride, moha-attachment, maatsarya – jealousy.

Bad: Only the boys (8-12 years old) of Brahmins, Kshatriyas and Vaishyas had the right to the ceremony of upanayana – supplementary eye of knowledge –also called the sacred thread ceremony. This was considered a second birth and these three varnas are termed dvija –twice born. This 'second birth' was originally open to dvija women, but was later denied. Only the dvija men were allowed to study Vedas. The gurukul system was meant only for the Brahmin and Kshatriya boys. The Vaishya boys were expected to learn the trade or the craft from their fathers.

Ugly: The freedom for persons to choose occupations befitting their inherent capabilities was lost. The varna was decided by birth alone and no change of varna was permitted. Intermarriages between varnas were prohibited, but did occur on a large enough scale. The progeny of mixed marriages of different kinds were segregated into jati (castes) within a class.

By about 200 BCE, the system had become rigid, and the number of jaties had increased manifold. By 1000 CE, the castes and sub-castes had further increased owing to the absorption of different immigrants into the Hindu fold. A fifth but officially non-recognized class of dasyus –menials, slaves – had been added. These were kept away from the main village dwellings and had almost no rights. The status of women was low, and their role was restricted to home making, cooking and rearing children. A woman was expected to be respected at home, but was expected to live with the support of the father, the husband and the son(s) in the three stages of life.

Around 1840, the British started educating the 'natives' in English with the twin objective of getting local persons to run the empire and of familiarizing them with the 'superior' British (European/Western) culture. By then, many bad practices had been strongly rooted among the Hindus. Some of the widespread were: child marriages for girls, education prohibited for girls and women, strict restrictions on widows of the dvija classes and no remarriages for these widows, considering about 15-20 percent of the population as untouchables, and preventing shoodras and untouchables from education. Among the infrequent were the practices of sati (self-emollition by the widowed wife at the funeral pyre of her dead husband); infant and other human sacrifices; and honor killings of girls for 'ruining the reputation of the family'; honor killing of girls/boys wedding out of caste. Several taboos had become traditional: not eating beef by all four classes, vegetarianism for most Brahmin castes, no crossing of seas by Brahmins and Kshatriyas, concepts of purity and impurity especially for the Brahmin class. The caste hierarchy had become extremely strong, with Brahmins/Kshatriyas at the top and the untouchables at the bottom. From time immemorial, the Brahmins had the responsibility of interpreting the scriptures and deciding the kind of laws that would apply to the Hindu society. So, the Brahmins continued to be in the forefront also in maintaining the traditions, good and bad; and their womenfolk were the worst sufferers.

A major consequence of the strong social discrimination and rigid rules among Hindus was conversion to Islam by those lower in social hierarchy. Islam offered equality to all within the religion. As a proselytizing religion, Islam forced conversion on many and induced many by offering financial advantages. Voluntary conversions without any inducement were few. Hinduism had become moribund; those who were converted forcibly and wished to come back into Hinduism were not allowed to do so. This situation prevailed over a period of over 700 years from around 1100 CE. As a result, about 25% of the population of British India (1946) was Muslim.

Jews first landed in Cochin in 70 BCE, were given safe asylum. Jews from many countries arrived in India in the next 1500 years and lived peacefully with Hindus. Christianity had arrived in Kerala, on the west coast of India, in 52 CE. These Christians had practiced their religion freely and had also proselytized somewhat. By the 600 CE, Christianity was well established. The Parsees from Persia landed in Surat in 900 CE. They, given full freedom to pursue their religion Zoroastrianism, also flourished. Jews and Parsees did not proselytize. The early Bahai's came in 1844 CE, but organized themselves as a separate religion during 1910-1920. In 2014, the largest population of Bahais in the world may be in India.

Christianity started spreading when Christian missionaries from Europe started preaching their religion in India from 1500. Catholic, Jesuit and Protestant missionaries became active during the 18th century and started schools and colleges all over India in the 19th century. Their efforts succeeded in converting many tribal groups and also many from the untouchable castes to Christianity. It needs to be emphasized that the British – East India Company and the British Crown – did not support the Christian missionaries. The Portuguese, ruling over pockets on the west coast, however, supported even forceful conversion. Hindus refused to accept the repentant back into Hinduism.

Christianity had been adapting itself to the changes brought about by the scientific method and the industrial revolution (1750). The activities of missionaries exposed Hindus to many 'new' ideas. A few educated Indians from the dvija varnas voluntarily converted to Christianity. Though not liked by the majority, not even one of them was ostracized, because Hinduism accepts many paths to God as valid.

The impact of the defective social organization of Hinduism and the efforts by the proselytizing religions is best seen from the first census of free India. In 1951, in a total population of about 360 millions, Hindus were about 85%, Muslims 9%, Sikhs 2.5%, Christians 2.5%, rest 1%. (About 75% of Muslims from British India went to Pakistan in 1947-48. Most of those who did not believe in the 'two-nation theory' and some others stayed.)

CHAPTER 3
Dharma: Several Paths

The scriptures of Hinduism are of three kinds: shruti, smruti and puraana. Besides these, the two epics Ramayana and Mahabharata are also revered. The Bhagavad-gita, a part of Mahabharata, is considered to be a scripture of Hinduism. Vedas, and their components like Upanishadas, are the 'revealed' scriptures –shruties. The societal laws formulated from time to time by the wise, like those by Manu, are smruties. And puranas, each devoted to a God, deal with ideas on creation and destruction of the world, genealogies and stories of gods and kings. Rituals of Hinduism often proclaim, " – as said in shruti, smruti, purana". The diversity of thoughts and concepts in these multiple scriptural sources is vast and mind boggling, but can be expressed clearly in the context of moksha -liberation.

Hindu thinkers realized that all people cannot be given one single path in their quest for *the truth* about the purpose of human life, and about the origin and existence of earth and the universe. They also realized that reason –human intelligence –may not be adequate to answer questions about God or about existence of life after death. They knew that 'faith' of any kind can be questioned and did not wish to suppress questioning. Therefore, their schema for arriving at moksha permits each person to choose a path that fits his/her personality. (See figure 3.1 on the next page).

Figure 3.1
Moksha (Liberation)
Three paths: same destination

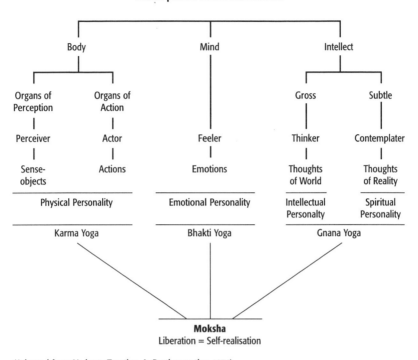

(Adapted from Vedanta Treatise, A. Parthasarathy, 1976)

The three basic philosophical concepts of Hinduism are aatma, samsaara, and moksha. Atma is roughly translated as soul; atma is indestructible, is the same stuff in all living beings, and goes into another body (not necessarily human) after death. Samsara stands for the cycle of birth and death of bodies, and rebirth of that atma in another body. The atma is bound to body from life to life, and moksha is the release of the atma from this cycle of births and rebirths. Moksha can come in many forms: it is union with the super soul – param-aatma – of which each soul is a part; it is realization that 'my atma is the same as parmamatma'; it is not being bound by the results of karma –action; it is utter devotion to God; it is freedom from the many dualities of life like happiness-sorrow; it is mental peace and serenity of the highest level. {The concepts of swarga (heaven) and naraka (hell) are mentioned in the puranas, but not in the Vedas. The soul is supposed to dwell in these places for a time decided by the doer's karma and then return for rebirth into a human or other form, again based on karma.}

Figure 3.1 above shows three paths to moksha, to be chosen according to the orientation of the individual: body, mind, or intellect. The body path –karma yoga – can be taken with or without the stipulations about soul, rebirth and god: detachment from the fruits of action leads to being free from mental disturbances. One is then not bound by the effects of karma. The mind path is of devotion –bhakti yoga –to a manifestation of the paramatma (also termed as brahman that is not describable) in human form; i.e. God in the image of man. Here, God is benevolent, omnipresent, omniscient and omnipotent: He (also She, in Hinduism) looks after His devotees and answers their prayers. Those who find an anthropomorphic God unacceptable on the basis of rationality can follow the third path -intellect – dnyana yoga. Those with intellectual leaning may follow the saankhya school of philosophy[@], where the Doer of an action is seen as only one of the five elements needed for work to happen.

[@] *How this 'philosophy of work' helps to groom self in humility and to eliminate mental stress is described in two books by Ashok R. Garde: Ch.18 of Chanakya on Management, Jaico 2006, and Ch 8 of Theory and Practice of Ethics and Morals, ICFAI University Press, 2010.*

These elements are: adhisthaan-basis, karta-doer, karan-means, cheshtaa-efforts and daiva-luck or chance. Those with spiritual inclination towards the unknowable entity –brahman –may take up the path of the Vedaanta philosophy, where one realizes that, "I am brahman". Some may follow the path of raajayoga, which is a step wise process leading to Samaadhi –the utterly serene (bliss) state of mind.

This schema is a truly generalized representation of human quest for the unknown. Anthropomorphic religions like Judaism, Zoroastrianism, Christianity, Islam, Shinto, Sikhism, and Baha'i are on the central path of devotion. Buddhism is aligned to the intellectual stream, while Jainism is more akin to the action –karma –stream. The animistic religions of the tribal world, animal and plant worship in Hinduism and Shinto get classed under the devotion stream because the manifestation of the unknowable super power –brahman - is in animal or plant form. The adherents of Confucianism, the atheists, the agnostics and the non-religionists can be considered on the path of intellect like the sankhya philosophy that is atheist or on the path of the karma that does not need God. Their moksha may be simply a serene state of mind, with no need for any assumptions about atman, brahman, re-birth or super power. Even the Vedanta philosophy is almost atheist: 'I cannot pray to God if I am brahman!'

Like other human parameters, even religiosity seems to be spread as the statistical distribution called 'normal': a bell shaped curve. A large proportion of humanity is found to follow anthropomorphic God –the bhaktiyoga; and that includes a large majority of Hindus within Hinduism. The followers of the paths of karma yoga and dnyana yoga may be estimated, at a guess, to be around 10 % each.

In many countries of the world, Islam swamped the existing religion(s) to become the sole religion: Iran, Iraq, Egypt, and Indonesia among others. The core strengths of Hinduism helped it to withstand the forceful onslaught of Islam: only about 25% got converted in 700 years.

The main theological threat to Hinduism came from Christianity, as mentioned earlier. Hinduism has been able to withstand the good pressure built by Christianity by reforming itself. A good measure of the success of these efforts over a century and half is that the percentage of Indian Christians was only 2.5% in 1951, in spite of conversion efforts by missionaries over 200 years.

Before describing the current status of Hinduism it is necessary to know how the 'bad' and the 'ugly' aspects of the social side of Hinduism were eliminated and how religious reforms were undertaken. Let us have a brief overview of how social justice was restored within Hinduism; and of the religious reforms.

CHAPTER 4
Dharma: Social Reforms

The first assault on the built-in inequality of the varna system came in the 10th century BCE from Lokaayata, Also known as the Chaarvaaka School of philosophy, Lokaayata did not accept the authority of Vedas and insisted with remarkable logic that, "only that which is perceived by the five senses is valid, not even inferences from observed facts." In their view, concepts such as soul, rebirth, and god are non-valid and unnecessary. *'Given the fact that birth and death take place for all living beings in nature, the right philosophy is to enjoy life as much as possible and try to reduce the unhappiness of all kinds. The varna system is a concoction of the Brahmins, and priesthood their way of earning a living. All men are created equal'.* About women, there seems to be no clarity in this philosophy, which is most likely to have considered them as equal partners in pursuit of happiness. It is to be noted that this philosophy was challenged, but those propounding it were neither persecuted nor boycotted. However, this non-believer system of thought gradually got extinct owing to the need of the general populace to believe in a protective God, and the consequent lack of followers of Lokayat. The varna-ashram system continued. The next assault came in the 7th century BCE from Jainism and Buddhism. Like the Lokayat, both rejected the authority of the Vedas, believed in rebirth, and considered all persons in society as equals. They welcomed all to become Saadhus and Bhikkhus respectively, irrespective of their varna. A little grudgingly, they also accepted women as Saadhvis and Bhikkhunis. All men were equal, but the women had an inferior status in the life of renunciation also. However, neither of these religions took upon themselves to eliminate the varna system then and the caste system later. Judaism and Zoroastrianism had entered India, but had no impact on Hinduism. Entrance of Islam on the Indian scene, first in 712 CE in the province of Sindh, started with giving Hindus a status equivalent to that given to the followers of the 'book religions' – Judaism and Christianity. This was a pragmatic decision not sanctioned by Qur'an, which had clearly stated that idol worshippers are kafirs. The only two options available for kafirs is conversion to Islam or death! After the Muslim rulers became Indian rulers from 1100 CE, the impact of Islam was large scale conversion of Hindus, through force or inducement. Again, pragmatic considerations led to letting the Hindus, always a majority in the population, live peacefully rather than to consider them as kafirs or make them also confirm to the Sharia laws. Hindus, under pressure from these rulers, became more protective of their social and religious systems and did not start any reforms by picking up some good points of Islam. Later, in 1500, the confrontation between Islam and Hinduism led to the establishment of a new religion - Sikhism. It was only the proselytizing efforts of the Christian missionaries and the opening up to the outside world through the English language in around 1830 that lead to a major effort to reform Hinduism. The wide gap between the theoretical equality of all atmas and the real life discrimination between men and women had to be bridged; the horrendous void between philosophy and practice had to be eliminated to make Hinduism internally consistent, fair and just.

The reform process from within Hinduism had started from the 11th century. A series of saint poets from the bhakti marga (path) had composed and sung songs in the languages of the people (over 18) in the next five centuries, till 1700. They brought home the basics of Hinduism to the masses via the stories of Gods Rama, Krishna, Shiva, Ganapati, Hanuman, and Goddess Durga. Their message was that all are children of the same God and will obtain moksha through good behavior. Their poetry, lyrics and message of love and compassion for all living beings are sung even in the 21st century. Their devotion to their God got them many followers and even the illiterate masses in all states of India became cognizant with several important features of their religion. Though the saint poets came from different castes of different varnas and their message from God was respected and revered, they could not go beyond their caste limits. The shoodra and the untouchable saints were not permitted to enter the temples of the God they praised! The upper castes often boycotted them during their lifetime, though revered them later owing for their great contributions to Hinduism. These saints could not and did not seek elimination of the caste distinctions and untouchability deeply rooted in all layers of the Hindu society.

The movements that started in 1810 and culminated in 1960 accomplished a complete conceptual overhaul of Hinduism. Persons educated in the new system established by the British (and thus conversant with English language and literature) undertook to reform one or more aspect of the Hindu social system and devoted their life for such work. Expectedly, the dvija varnas (Brahmins, Kshatriyas, and also some Vaishya categories) who were reared in the tradition of 'learning' in the Hindu society, were the first to acquire such education. Several shoodra and some untouchables were lucky to get opportunity to acquire such education, owing to the support of enlightened British and Hindu leaders and of Hindu rulers of princely states. Starting with Ram Mohan Roy in Bengal, Swami Dayanand Saraswati of Punjab and Jyotirao Phule, M G Ranade of Maharashtra, these reform movements spread into all provinces of India. Most of the items on the agenda of reform were tackled between 1830 and 1890. These were the same as listed earlier under the sub-heading 'Ugly' in Chapter 1: eradicating child marriage, giving education to girls and women, encouraging young widows of dvijas for remarriage (this was practiced by the shoodras and the others traditionally), establishing the right for women to learn a vocation and to earn for a living, providing asylum for children born out of wedlock, providing homes for women driven out from families, eliminating caste discrimination and untouchability. Visiting the hamlets of untouchables, inviting them for meals, teaching them to read and write, fighting against the concept of 'impurity' of contacts with the untouchable or a shoodra (or with a mlencha –Muslim or a yavana –European, especially for the Brahmins). Some of these continued till 1930s while some new items were added. The other social reforms were: to eliminate the system of dowry (money given by the bride's side to the groom's side at marriage time), denounce and prevent the corresponding dowry deaths of young brides, tolerate or even encourage inter-caste marriages, advocate methods of birth control, increase literacy of adult men and women of 'lower' castes. Each of these reformers, irrespective of his/her caste, had to face strong opposition from the orthodox men and women of all castes, especially of the dvija castes. Even among the shoodra castes and the untouchable communities, the fear of retribution was extremely strong and real. In the initial stages only the morally courageous among the lower castes joined the movements towards equality and liberty for all. The reformers were ridiculed, threatened, pelted with stones and cow dung in public, sometimes beaten with sticks, boycotted from community. Invariably, no reformer replied in kind. In each province individuals and groups worked for different causes; there was no central all-India planning or control. The leaders of these groups visited other provinces, propagated their cause, helped establish similar groups or organizations and mutually supported each other as they saw fit. The reformers adopted a very pragmatic and correct stance that most of the practices they wanted to change had no support from the main scriptures shrutis, i. e. the Vedas. They knew that several traditions, especially the varna-caste based differentiation, originated in the smruties. They pointed out that smruties are man-made (not 'revealed' like the Vedas) and they need to change with time. Here, the philosophical underpinning of atma being the same for all living beings and the work of saint poets came to their help, directly and indirectly. They continued their task of changing the mindset of the Hindu populace, especially of the upper caste dvijas, patiently over their lifetime. They established a large number of trusts and societies under the Societies Act passed by the British Government in 1860. This institution building not only strengthened their respective cause but also ensured continuity over long periods. Many organizations wound up after the cause they promoted became a normal practice, many are continuing in the 21st century and all of these are now open to the needy irrespective of their religion.

We thus see that all this progress toward equality of opportunity and liberty for all men and women among the Hindus took a great toll of painful and persevering efforts over 150 years by a large number of dedicated men and women from within Hinduism. The opposition to social reforms had come also from another direction: many during the years 1900 to 1930 were of the opinion that social reforms should be given a lower priority over the struggle for independence against the British. Fortunately, both progressed simultaneously.

Social reforms need legal and political support for their success. Many laws were enacted by the British government to support changes that needed legal support for surer and faster implementation. Examples are the laws preventing infant killing (1810), making sati a legal offence (1830) and setting the minimum age of marriage (1910). Political support was essential to eliminate caste based societal hierarchy and to give political strength to those who were deprived for centuries. The first elections to provincial and federal/central government in 1936-7 under the British saw democracy in action. One vote was given to each person, men and women, irrespective of their religion and caste. However, only about 15% of the population was considered eligible for voting, about 46% of seats were non-general (reserved) of which about 30% seats were reserved for the Muslims. The very first affirmative action in support of the 'lower castes' by any government was taken in 1902 by the Hindu ruler of the princely state of Kolhapur in Maharashtra. He reserved 50% of the jobs in government for the non-dvija castes, and made education for all their boys and girls free and compulsory. In a similar vein, the Hindu princely states of Indore, Baroda and Mysore, among others, passed several laws during 1910 to 1940; minimum age for marriage, permitting widows to marry, helping education of girls, giving property rights to women etc. However, real political empowering of the downtrodden – dalit, as they preferred to call themselves collectively – took place only after India gained independence in 1947. The constitution of free India (1950) declared Bhaarat (official name of India) as a secular democracy with a federal structure for government. It gave all men and women the right to vote, and the right to equal opportunity irrespective of religion, caste and class. Untouchability was banned and practicing it became a punishable offence. More importantly, the constitution took affirmative action to reserve seats in educational institutes and in government jobs for those sections of the society that were deprived of these for over 2000 years. The castes identified for such purposes were termed as Scheduled Castes and the tribal groups earmarked for this were termed the Scheduled Tribes. The quota for SC was 15% and that for ST was 7.5% based on their respective population in the 1931 census. This reservation was meant for the first five years, but has been extended continually. Later, in 1990s, the Other Backward Classes –OBC - were also added to this list, taking the total reservation to 52.5 %. This political empowerment and the processes of affirmative action have played a major role in making the Hindu society fair and just to all within their fold, in principle. A very small minority may continue to defend the old order of caste hierarchy and of inferior status of women, but a very large majority of Hindus accept the concept of equality and liberty. However, complete elimination of such distinctions has not been possible in practice.

In retrospect, the entire process of social reforms in Hinduism can be seen as a movement of the traditional Hindu society bound by old morals to a modern Hindu society adhering to ethics. Moral ideas are formed from early childhood: the views of mother, father, family, religion, school, and community influence the person and determine his/her moral stances. Moral tenets are invariably accepted involuntarily first, their rationalized justification follows later. Moral tenets, therefore, are culture specific and thus also are dependent upon the period in history. Ethics has been precisely defined: (Please see footnote on p22). "Let a person A take an action X that makes him (her) happy. If the action X affects another person B, and if the person B were to take the same action X affecting A, will A continue to be happy? If YES, then the action X is ethical" Example: "I am happy to steal money from someone, but if that someone steals from me, I am unhappy! Therefore, stealing is unethical." Thus, ethics is universally applicable to all human communities irrespective of the period in history. Every moral tenet, irrespective of its source, needs to be tested to determine whether it is also ethical. The ethically acceptable tenets are worth adopting in society; those ethically neutral may be adopted or tolerated. Those found ethically unacceptable need to be rejected. Depending upon the severity and spread of such ethically bad moral tenets, the actions to be taken would be persuasion, education or even legal prevention. We note that the Hindu society has followed such a course to eliminate the ethically unacceptable (but were once morally justified either by citing authority of smrutis or as strong traditions) social practices.

CHAPTER 5
Dharma: A Reaffirmation

The social practices sanctioned by Hinduism, based primarily on the Manu-smruti written in 200 BCE, and also on traditions of obscure origin, needed to be re-examined in the 19th century. A similar scrutiny had to be given to the philosophical and theological aspects of Hinduism by the Hindu thinkers at that time. The Christian missionaries were making great efforts to show that Hinduism is not a religion of the right kind and therefore, the 'pagan' Hindus must convert to Christianity for their salvation. Their conclusion about the nature of Hinduism was understandable, because the common Hindu was not in a position to explain the 'why' behind the 'how' of his religious practices and rituals. Also, the Europeans that came in contact with India in the beginning of the 18th century could neither see the wide variety of religious practices of the Hindus as of 'one religion' nor were they aware of the great cultural heritage of the Hindus. The situation changed in the latter half of the 19th century. A number of Western scholars studied the Sanskrit language and translated the Vedas and the Upanishadas into French, German and English. These scholars – Indologists - opened the doors to Sanskrit literature: the epics Ramayana and Mahabharata; Bhagavad-gita; poems and plays; treatises on drama, dance, mathematics, astronomy, sculpture and many others. By the beginning of the 20th century, this opening up of Sanskrit literature had changed the perception of the West about Hindus and their ancient Indian civilization.

Christianity has several features that are attractively inviting: only one God, no idol worship, orientation for helping the poor or the destitute, and an organized Church with congregations praying together in a solemn atmosphere. Several educated Indians studied the Bible, and a few intellectuals converted willingly to Christianity. This was a different phenomenon than one involved in the conversion of the shoodras, untouchables and the tribal groups. Altogether, the forces acting towards conversion to Christianity were correctly perceived as a threat to Hinduism. By the middle of the 19th century, the enlightened among Hindus had come out of the subjugated mentality of the conquered. They had become assertive on the political, social and religious fronts.

The only right way to protect Hinduism was to introspect, to analyze, and to bring in the right kind of reforms in religious practices, wherever necessary, from within Hinduism. In retrospect, the steps that were then taken can be considered to be of eight types: to adapt good ideas from Christianity by demonstrating that these are covered in Hindu scriptures, to explain the philosophical basis, to bring out the rationale behind the meaningful practices of Hinduism, to eliminate some non-essential rituals and to give less importance to some rituals, to reconsider ideas on purity-impurity, to eliminate irrational taboos and the corresponding atonement procedures, to avoid outward signs of dress and gait up indicating caste differences, and to encourage congregational activities within Hinduism.

The first result of the re-examination of Hinduism in the context of Christianity was the establishment of the Braahmo

Samaaj (Ram Mohan Roy) in (Calcutta) Kolkata, Bengal in 1828; the Praarthana Samaj (Justice M.G. Ranade) in 1867 and the Arya Samaj (Swami Dayanand Saraswati) in 1875, both in (Bombay) Mumbai, Maharashtra. Essentially, all three went back to the Vedas. They did not approve idol worship at homes or in temples since idol worship is not a 'revealed truth' of the Vedas. These samaj were established city wise in many parts of India over the next century. These reformers worked for removing the caste distinctions, opened up the studies of Vedas to non-Brahmins, supported women studying the Vedas and simplified several rituals. They encouraged people to come together for prayers at public halls. They believed in karma, rebirth and moksha, but not in an anthropomorphic God. Prarthana Samaj was theistic and encouraged its followers to sing the verses from Marathi saint poets. The Arya Samaj took lead in re-converting to Hinduism those Hindus who wished to come back from Islam or from Christianity. Arya Samaj also welcomed persons from other religions to become Hindu, both moves unprecedented in the history of Hinduism.

The philosophical basis of Hinduism was explicitly brought to the people by organizations like the Ramkrishna Math and Ramkrishna Mission (1897) established by Swami Vivekananda, and by Vedanta Societies as its arm in the USA. The concepts of nirguna brahman –the non-describable super power – and that of a saguna brahman – God in the image of man –were shown to be two sides of the same coin. Self-Realization Fellowship (Parmahansa Yogananda) was established in the USA in 1920 to spread the message of Kriya Yoga and spiritual development through meditation. Later, in 1953, Chinmaya Mission (Swami Chinmayanada) was established to propagate the ideas of Vedanta world over. Essentially, the six philosophical schools of Hinduism and the three paths of moksha were explained by the monks of these and such other organizations. They demonstrated the way in which these philosophies can be converted into practice that brings freedom and bliss to the followers. Since Hinduism accepts all paths to God as good, none of these organizations insist that their followers convert to Hinduism for practicing their recommendations.

The concept of saguna brahman leads to accepting that brahman can manifest itself in different forms which are easy to understand for the common man; namely, in the form of a personalized God. This God manifests in essentially four forms: the creator –Brahma, the sustainer –Vishnu, and the destroyer –Mahesh and the Goddess of strength –Durga. Each has many names, forms and incarnations; and many other Gods form part of their family or retinue. A Hindu becomes a devotee of any manifestation either because of his family or community tradition, and can also choose a different one or more than one deity any time. Essentially, every Hindu knows that ultimately there is only ONE GOD –the brahman or the paramatma; and prayer to any God goes ultimately to the same ONE GOD. Two well-known sayings were made common knowledge: 'Like water from all rivers ends up in the sea, bowing to any God ends up in bowing to THE GOD.' And 'The truth is only ONE; wise men speak of it in different ways.' Several sects or smapradaayas of Hinduism, each following either Vishnu or Shiva or Durga as their main deity, were leading people on the bhakti path in several streams since around 200 BCE. Additions to these have been continuously made till the present times (20th century). The fact that each of these deities is a specific manifestation of the saguna brahman was emphasized to bring out the unity in their diversity.

The daily and periodic rituals prescribed by the Manusmruti of 200 BCE were not meaningful for the daily life of individuals living in the industrialized society that values equality and liberty. The Brahmins, for example, were expected to perform five sacrifices per day, starting early morning and ending at dusk. These were not being performed by most Brahmins since long; only the morning sandhya –salutation to sun god – and possibly the evening sandhya - were being performed in the 19th century. The sanskaras – religious ceremonies –meant for dvija varnas from conception to death of an individual were as many as sixteen. Only about eight were being followed, mostly by dvijas only. The reformers rationalized the rituals by ignoring many and considered only the four related to the naming ceremony of the child, the upanayan ceremony for the dvijas entering brahmacharya-ashram from balya stage, the marriage ceremony and the death rituals as important sanskaras. Except the marriage ceremony, all others were considered voluntary; those who did not perform them were tolerated. The marriage ceremony, though somewhat different in the different language based territories of India, was very elaborate, and its duration could be as many as three days. This ceremony has been simplified by keeping the essential parts that deal with the relationships between the husband and wife, their families and the society. Similarly, the elaborate death ritual was simplified, without sacrificing the reverence it showed for the ancestors. Many a superstitious traditions that had grown around these rituals were gradually eliminated. All these steps were taken by showing how they are consistent with the principles of Hinduism as seen from shruti-smruti-puranas. Even so, considerable resistance was faced by such reformers, mostly Brahmins, from the entrenched priesthood, also consisting of Brahmins. As late as in the 1970s, Dnyaan Prabodhini, a social reform organization in Maharashtra, has simplified these rituals and has encouraged persons form other than Brahmin community and also women to take up priesthood for conducting worships and rituals.

Many ideas on shoucha – ashoucha (purity –impurity) had a strong influence on the minds of men and women of the dvija varnas, mainly among the Brahmins. An impurity could arise by touching a forbidden thing or a person, by allowing forbidden persons into the household (especially into the kitchen), because women undergo monthly period of menses, because a woman had delivered a baby, by attending any funeral, because of the death of specified near relatives, and by many other kinds of events. One could absolve oneself from most of such 'faults of impurity' by taking a bath. When things became impure, they had to be sprinkled with water from the holy river Ganga (Ganges) or with the holy cow-urine. An impurity like the woman in menses or person in sutak – impurity owing to death of near relative - were non-removable and the persons concerned had to wait a specified number of days of seclusion akin to quarantine before they could become 'normal' again. Tradition had also brought in other such paired concepts: shubha - ashubha (good - bad omen); punya –paap (holy deed-sin).Cutting nails on Saturdays would be bad omen, feeding grass to a cow or a dip in the river Ganges would be a punya (holy deed) and sitting together with a shoodra would be a papa (sin) etc. As the movements for social reforms started making their impact and as education among women increased, most of these ideas disappeared. Ideas from science, availability of new technology and compulsions of industrialization where men and women started working together changed the scenario gradually.

Many of the moral tenets from smrutis and from traditions of uncertain origins were about forbidding certain type of behavior. Certain items of food were forbidden, meat-fish was forbidden to most Brahmin castes, shaving or hair cutting was not to be done on certain days of the week, not travelling toward the south on certain days, not sleeping with feet toward south, and many such relatively insignificant restrictions were prevalent. More hurting were the taboo on crossing seas and the strict prohibition on killing a cow or on eating beef. Although beef eating has not been forbidden in any shruti or smruti, it was forbidden traditionally and the cow had become holy to the Hindus. By itself, this taboo or holiness of the cow were not disturbing: but the Muslims often put the Hindus down by deliberately killing cows and eating beef etc. The taboo on seafaring was fortunately not common for all Hindus, and was more for the Brahmins and Kshatriyas. For each breaking of such moral dictum, either knowingly or unknowingly, a specific atonement procedure was prescribed. A person could absolve himself from the dosha –fault, or a mild form of sin – of having done the prohibited. Most of these prohibitions have been given up: fasting or not eating meat for religious purposes continues, and so does the holy-ness of the cow. It is worth noting that most of the ideas on impurity and on prohibitions were ethically neutral. Obviously, these behaviors were such that when person A did these X actions, no person B was really affected.

An important factor that emphasized the caste differences amongst Hindus was the person's appearance. The style of dress, the head gear and the facial features were different for each caste. The Brahmin men, for example, had to shave the head except for keeping a shikhaa – a bundle of hair at the top-back of head- and wear a certain type of pagadi – a head gear made from a long piece of cloth, but removable like a cap. All dvija men who had undergone the upanayana –sacred thread - ceremony had to wear the sacred thread all through their life. The women needed to wear kumkum –a red dot – on their forehead. The widowed women had to shave completely, were prohibited from wearing kumkum and mangalsutra –a special necklace signifying a married woman - and were expected to wear only red saris or only white saris. The men had to keep mustache and were permitted to remove it only after father's death. The women were prohibited from wearing any dress other than saris in most of India, and other than salwar-khameez –somewhat like narrow pajama and large long shirt - in the northern and north western parts. All such restrictions were gradually removed; the trend towards using western style of clothing helped in a big way. Dress and personal appearance were delinked from Hinduism and became a matter of choice for individuals.

Hinduism does not expect any uniformity in the way an individual follows it. Unlike Christianity or Islam, no weekly visit by all adherents to a nearby temple at a stipulated time is ordained. A Hindu prays at home, or goes to a temple as and when he or she feels like. Consequently, praying together in congregations was not a routine occurrence. Such a practice was started by the Brahmo, Arya and Prarthana Samaj, but did not continue for long. Their place has been taken by satsang – company of good people who love God –groups of many denominations. A saintly person leading normal life is mostly the giver of such discourse to small groups of around 20-40. There existed a system of keertana – a religious bard speaking on a chosen topic of morals in prose and singing verses with actions – where men and women would gather, but sit segregated, in temples. In provinces like Gujarat, the festival of navraatri –nine nights –was celebrated by the masses where men and women come together and dance in praise of the Goddess Ambaa/Durgaa. Several 'holy places' all over India had specific days of the year when a festival to pray for a particular deity was held annually. In many parts of the country Hindu devotees came together and travelled on foot to a holy place up to 200 km away. Such congregations and pilgrimages were encouraged. Moreover, many saintly figures, both men and women, took upon themselves to give public discourses on different topics of Hinduism such as from the Bhaagawat Purana or the Bhagawadgita. The audiences for such discourses for men and women together can be from about 100 to 2000.

In spite of the bleak future predicted by several Western scholars about Hinduism, the Hindu reformers have achieved what appeared to be nearly impossible in the beginning of the 19th century. Hinduism has changed so drastically that the Hindus born after 1960s have little or no feel about the tremendous constraints exerted by the traditions of Hinduism around 1800 CE. They are just not aware of the task that was involved in reforming Hinduism on the social and religious fronts. Most take the current format for granted, which is a good sign. They should know that the core concepts of Hinduism were also examined in this process of reforms and were found to need no change. Hindus have been able to assert what has been claimed since the birth of Hinduism; that their religion is eternal -sanatana dharma. A glimpse of this was given in Chapter 3 on paths to moksha.

The social reforms described in the previous chapter 4 and the religious reforms illustrated in this chapter 5 have made Hinduism a religion suited to the modern times defined by the great impact of technological progress. As seen earlier, Hinduism is a religion that has shown its adaptability to changing circumstances since olden times dating back to 1000 BCE. The changes brought about since 1800 AD are not solely because of the threat from Christianity. Seen from another viewpoint, Hinduism has adapted itself to the changed environment brought by the progress of science and technology leading to industrialization on a large scale in India. In fact, Christianity has changed similarly over the period of 1600 to 2000 CE. The Bible, which originally spoke only to Brothers, has been speaking to Brothers and Sisters since long; several Christian sects [and even the Pope in 1994) have accepted that 'other religious paths' can lead to God. Slavery, apparently not ostracized in the Bible, finds no mention today. Christianity, too, has been adopting an ethical stance in preference to a rigid moral stance (examples: accepting divorce, homosexuality, unmarried mothers). The march of world religions from morals to ethics is a good sign of progress of humanity toward the ideals of equality and liberty for all humans. We will see many more examples of this phenomenon as we look at Hinduism in the 21st century. It can be safely predicted that Hinduism will adapt continually to reformulate itself for the good of mankind over the coming centuries.

The next Chapter 6 deals with the core concepts of Hinduism and the philosophies underlying its practices, both of which needed no change at all during the process of reform. We also take a fresh look at the three dimensional structure for the individual in society as it needs to be seen and understood after the social reforms.

Dharma: Modernized Hinduism

No religion permits its scriptures to be edited and re-written for any reason whatever, and Hinduism is no exception. The Vedas are shrutis – the revealed basic scriptures that include the Upanishadas –and so are sacrosanct. Similarly, the text of Bhagawadgita, the dialogue between the God Krishna and his disciple, cannot be changed. If these texts contain ideas that are seen to be inapplicable in the modern world, then those can be simply left as they are but not put into practice. Fortunately, the smrutis are meant to be compiled afresh by the wise to suit the changing times. Therefore, the ethical transformation painstakingly brought about during 1800 to 2000 CE can as well be seen as a development of a new smruti - societal rules. This new smruti is appropriate for the world transformed through science, technology, and industrialization, and also through democracy with free market economy. Let us now turn to the core concepts of modernized Hinduism and its new smruti. Both will be seen to be valid for centuries to come.

Core Concepts

1. The basic concepts of Hinduism are atma, brahman or pramatma, karma, rebirth, samsara and moksha. Atma (soul) is immortal, has no beginning or end, and is like the paramatma (supersoul) or brahman, which is the indescribable formless entity that makes existence of

universe possible. Atma takes on a body of a living being, is bound by the karma (actions) of the body and when the body dies, it is bound to enter another body. This cycle of births and deaths of bodies and perpetuation of atma is termed samsara. Moksha –release – is the release of the atma from sansara –the cycle of deaths and births. Only very evolved atmas, after a large number of cycles of births and deaths, get the human body. Humans, with discretion to act the right way, need to perform the right types of karma to overcome the effects of karmas from the past life and to go nearer to the stage of moksha. As and when the karmas are performed in a way that they do not bind the atma, the atma is released from the bondage of samsara. The goal of every human life is such release - moksha.

It may be noted that Jainism, Buddhism and Sikhism also have similar beliefs about karma, samsara and moksha; but these do not consider Vedas as their sacred texts. Thus, Hinduism distinguishes itself from them by its veda-praamaanya –by taking Vedas as valid scriptures.

2. The three paths to moksha –karma, bhakti and dnyana margas or yogas –are another core concept of Hinduism, which is the most democratic religion of the world. Depending upon the nature of a person, he or she can choose any of these paths or its sub-path. These concepts (Chapter 3) needed no change whatever owing to their universality. Those following the karma yoga paths of the perceiver or the actor may or may not need to think in terms of samsara. They may seek bliss through simply doing their work with total involvement and playing their roles well in life, without being 'attached' to the fruits of their work,

accepting favorable and unfavorable results with equanimity. Those on the intellect based paths of the thinker or the contemplator would find the concept of samsara worthwhile, since it gives more opportunity than just one life to reach the ultimate destination of moksha. For them, moksha is union of atma and paramatma or the realization that atma is paramatma. Neither of these paths of karma and dnyana needs an anthropomorphic God. Those who are on the path of bhakti are those who prefer the saguna manifestation of brahman; an anthropomorphic God who is omniscient, omnipotent and benevolent. Once the possibility of the indescribable brahman manifesting as God is accepted, Hinduism accepts multiplicity of such manifestations as logical. Therefore, Hinduism has many Gods and Goddesses, each with different focus of activities. A devotee chooses the God or the Goddess that he/she finds satisfying his/her yearning for a 'last resort'. The devotion is non-exclusive: it can extend to one or more other God/Goddess. A large majority of Hindus follow the bhakti marga, and even those from the other two paths of karma and dnyana do not show any repugnance to the bhakti path. All are aware that all paths can lead to moksha. We will look at the implications of bhakti marga in detail in Chapter 7 later, under the topic 'Practice of Hinduism'.

However, these ideas of brahman manifesting in anthropomorphic form, of the oneness of all gods, of the unification of the Vedic gods and of the saguna bhakti gods are not just a theoretical juxtaposition by the gurus teaching dharma. All these ideas are embodied in specific prayers or hymns for any god. As example, let us take the very peculiar manifestation known world over as the Elephant

God of Hinduism, Ganesha. Ganesha is the son of Shiva and Parvati, brother of Kartikeya (Subramaniam in South India). The hymns for God Ganesha - ganapati-atharva-sheersha, in Sanskrit –are recited regularly by a large number of religiously educated Hindus. The reciter addresses Ganesha in many ways while seeking protection, intellectual strength and bliss. Some are given below as illustrations. The same philosophy holds good for each manifestation of God.

"You are brahman itself personified; you are the maker (Brahma), the maintainer (Vishnu), the destroyer Mahesh); you are the atman, the brahman in visible form; you are Indra, Rudra, Varuna, Vayu, Agni (all Vedic gods of nature); you are knowledge personified, you are beyond the three gunas (personal characteristics); you are eternal bliss."

3. The basic prayers of Hinduism, oft repeated in the Upanishadas, are of two kinds: a person seeking on his own, and the guru and shishya –the teacher and the pupil – seeking together.

"From untruth, lead me to truth. From darkness, lead me to light. From death, lead me to immortality."

"Let the two of us be protected. Let the two of us enjoy (life) together. Let the two of us commit acts of bravery. Let the learning of the two of us be brilliant; let the two of us not hate anyone."

Each of these prayers starts with the holy syllable 'aum' and ends with a wish for peace – shaantih - expressed three times for emphasis.

Consistent with the core concepts of Hinduism, no god is explicitly mentioned in these prayers. Followers of any of the three paths can use these prayers appropriately. Moreover, what is sought is something that is a general wish of humans toward a good life: enlightenment, peaceful collective life, and freedom from the fear of death that is an inevitable part of life. (In fact, any person of any religion may use these prayers as if the appeal is to the God of his/her religion.)

4. Another verse, totally secular, is also a part of daily prayers in Hinduism since long.

"May all here (in this world) be happy, may all be healthy, may all see good (aspects of life and of people) and may none beget sorrow"

These are good wishes for the mankind (all living beings, including animals and plants), to be said by each person every day to remind him/her that the happiness of one is invariably dependent on happiness of others. It is easy to see 'bad' of others and around us, more difficult to see the 'good' that surrounds us in several ways. We note that no appeal is made here to any superpower.

Core Philosophies

Six schools of philosophies are at the base of Hinduism. These are termed aastik, i.e. they accept Vedas as scriptural authority: Saankhya, Yoga, Nyaaya, Vaisheshika, Mimaansa and Vedaanta. The other three schools, mentioned earlier in another context, are naastik, i.e. they do not accept Vedas: Lokayat, Jain and Buddhist. Later, Shaiva school was added to the aastik list and the importance of Nyaya and Vaisheshika schools reduced considerably. The Mimansa and Vedanta sort of merged, and only four main schools are now prevalent: Sankhya, Yoga, Vedanta and Shaiva. We will briefly review the core contents of the astik seven and see how they form an underpinning for Hinduism. These philosophies lead to practices that lie on one of the three/five paths to moksha - liberation.

Saankhya: Stipulates two irreducible, innate and independent entities: purusha –atma or consciousness, an entity that exists eternally – and prakriti –creative energy, materiality, and nature. Prakriti consist of three dispositions - gunas: sattva – rajas and tamas, translated loosely as harmony, activity, and inactivity. The imbalance between these three causes the world to evolve from prakriti. Purusha, the eternal, identifies itself with manas -mind, buddhi –intellect and ahankar- ego principle. Once the purusha realizes that it is different from prakriti, the purusha becomes free from samsara –the cycle of births and deaths. Saankhya philosophy of work says that work - karma - takes place due to five elements: adhishthaan - basis, kartaa- doer, karan- means, cheshtaa - efforts, and daiva- chance. The doer does not have total control on results. Practitioners of this atheistic philosophy fall on the path of Karmayoga or Dnyanayoga.

Yoga: Also known as Raajayoga, this philosophy aims at letting the 'seer' –aatman –to beget a state where he is in his 'true form'. The interval between the mind-waves is increased to lead to a stage termed samaadhi, which is a state of tranquility and bliss. A path of eight steps is prescribed to attain samadhi: yama (restraints) – niyama(observances) –

aasana (postures)- pranaayaama (control of breath) – pratyaahaara (withdrawal)–dhyaana (concentration)– dhaaranaa (meditation) –Samadhi (bliss). The techniques of yogic postures, pranayama and meditation belong to this philosophy. Ishwar – god –is defined as 'a person free from the effects of karma'. The practitioners fall on the thinkers' path of dnyana marga.

Nyaaya: This school uses a logical methodology to establish valid knowledge. There are only four sources of knowledge: pratyaksha –perception, anumaana –inference, upamaana – comparison and aagama –testimony. Since knowledge so obtained can be valid or false, several criteria have been developed to establish true validity. This methodology has · been used by others, but refuted by the Lokayat School.

Vaisheskika: This school postulates that anu –atoms - are the basic element, and brahman is the cause of consciousness in living beings. Reality is postulated as consisting of nine classes: four anu -atoms (earth, water, light and air), aakash –space, dik –direction, atman - infinity of souls- and manas - mind. The eternal individual souls pervade bodies for some time. Realization of this truth is liberation.

Mimaansa: The purpose of this school was to establish the authority of the Vedas as inviolable. They formulated rules for interpretation of Vedas. Performance of yajdnyas – sacrifices - as prescribed by the Vedas is the only way to moksha. Many Hindu rituals and ceremonies owe their origin to this school.

Vedaanta: Brahman is the only reality and the appearance of the world is the superimposition of maayaa –illusion - on brahman. There are three different schools within the Vedanta philosophy based on Upanishadas: advaita -non -dualism, dvaita -dualism and vishishthadvaita - qualified dualism, where the one-ness or separation of atman from parmatamn or brahman is involved. Truth is the realization that "I am brahman", or "I have achieved brahman state". Followers fall on the spiritual path of dnyana marga.

Shaiva: The created world is divided into two segments, insentient or the unconscious and sentient or the conscious, the soul. The insentient is divided into 13 causes and 10 effects, where causes include the 5 organs each of perception and action, three internal organs, intellect, ego principle and cognition principle. The causes are responsible for identification of self with non-self; liberation is union of the soul with God Shiva via intellect. Followers of this philosophy fall on the thinker's path to moksha – liberation.

Even such brief descriptions of these well-developed and extensively discussed schools of philosophy, (and their sub-schools, not indicated) bring out two basic facts. Firstly, the postulates of atma, samsara and moksha are accepted by all and secondly, there is no compulsive insistence on accepting only one set of ideas as valid, to the exclusion of others. Considerable latitude is given to independent thoughts without any suppression of dissidence. We note that these philosophies constitute the underpinning of Hinduism, which happens to be the only world religion so clearly based on philosophical thinking.

It is pertinent to note that only a small percentage of Hindus are familiar with these philosophies and only a fraction from these try to practice any of these philosophies that appeals to them. As mentioned earlier, an estimated 10-20 percent of the religiously knowledgeable Hindus practice these philosophies falling on the paths of karma and dnyana. The claim of Hinduism is that a seeker of moksha can indeed have a live experience of the infinite indescribable brahman using any of the three margas or paths. However, there exists a wide gap between cognitively understanding the philosophy of brahman and experiencing it within oneself as reality. It has been said since long," Only one in thousands of persons attempts to acquire siddhis (end results of yogic and other philosophy based practices); but only a few among those, who so attempt, succeed in *knowing* the brahman in principle." Since philosophies are abstract and somewhat difficult to understand and use in daily life, most people turn to the saguna bhakti marga. A very large majority of Hindus follow the bhakti path of saguna brahman where an anthropomorphic manifestation of God is omnipresent: one can worship such a God, pray for own well-being and seek help when in distress. The most visible practice of Hinduism is this bhakti marga. The diverse ways in which Hindus practice their religion will be covered in the next chapter, after describing the way in which the role of an individual in society is perceived in modern Hinduism as we enter the 21st century.

Individual in Society

We now give a fresh look to the three dimensional Hindu social structure that is not found in any other religion of the world: 4 occupation classes, 4 stages of life,and 4 goals of life. (See Chapter 2)

The varna had deteriorated into a rigid caste structure where birth decided the occupation and inter-caste social relations were prohibited. This caste system was considered by many Indologists to be so intricately intertwined with Hinduism, that a casteless society of Hindus was considered impossible. Since equal opportunity for education and liberty to choose vocation for all men and women have now been accepted within Hinduism, the caste is no barrier, theoretically. Superiority of a varna has no basis now, in principle, since a shoodra or a woman can be a priest. We have already seen that men and women in each of these four occupational classes have reached pinnacles of fame and are revered by the masses for their accomplishment. Substantial progress has been achieved towards removal of all caste barriers; much more needs to be done. But the concept of varna continues to make sense: each society needs thinkers-priests-teachers-scientists; people in defense services and police; wealth generators in agriculture and industry; and those who provide services of all kinds schools, hospitals, entertainment, sports. Any Hindu man or woman can choose to go to any of these classes –varnas. Why does one need such a formal structure for occupations at all? The answer within Hinduism lies in the expectations about the personal qualities of people in these four different varnas. The Brahmins by occupation, i. e. all those engaged in teaching, research, religious preaching etc., are expected to be knowledge oriented, to consider money as secondary motive for their work, and be able to control their anger and desires, be contented and peace-loving. The Kshatriyas –persons in defense services, police, judiciary and government etc. – are expected to be brave, courageous, with a sense of power to rule, and willingness to donate. The Viashyas –agriculturists, industrialists, traders –must go after wealth creation ethically and ensure that they share their wealth equitably with those who help them in their enterprise, and also share their wealth with the society. The Shoordras – those in services, entertainment, sports – need to be dedicated to their work, be sincere in meeting the needs of those whom they serve or entertain. Hindu religious texts, like other religious texts, are not expected to deal with the aspect of wealth generation, though the desirability of wealth is accepted by having God Kubera for money and Goddess Laxmi for wealth. The Hindu thinking on this aspect becomes clear when we consider the training given by Brahmin gurus to Kshatriya rulers in vogue since around 1000 BCE till 1700 CE among the Hindu rulers. The first known proponent of this system of training, Acharya (teacher) Chanakya (ca 320 BCE), starts his training program with the following six sutras (aphorisms)

"Happiness is rooted in ethics; Ethics is rooted in resources; Resources are rooted in kingdom (enterprise); Enterprise is rooted in self-control; Self-control is rooted in moral training; Moral training is rooted in serving with the elders (mentorship)"

Pursuit of happiness is a common goal for all in society. Ethical behavior by all in society is a necessary (but not sufficient) condition for all in the society to be happy. Unless the basic amenities of livelihood are available to all in society, it is not feasible to expect that all should behave ethically. Therefore, enterprise needs to be encouraged to produce wealth and to share it equitably with all others. Both the tasks, generating wealth and sharing wealth, depend upon the ethical behavior of those who generate wealth. So, the wealth generators and the rulers need to possess tremendous amount of self-control to be able to follow the path of ethics, which can be learnt with guidance from mentors.

This is the way in which the first three of the 4 purusharthas of the Z-axis are to be understood. Dharma –ethics –must be ever present when thinking of artha –resource generation - and kama –fulfillment of desires. Hinduism is a religion that encourages good life for all, while still keeping them aware of the ultimate goal of life, moksha–liberation. Even when engaged in pursuit of happiness through wealth generation and satisfaction of desires, the idea of detachment from all this is to be kept alive.

The X-axis of 4 periods of life tells us more about how best this is done. The learning opportunity during the Brahmacharya - ashrama, now available to all men and women, lets them educate themselves to their full capacity in areas they like. Depending upon the vocation, a person is ready to start wealth generation and family life earliest by 18 years of age, and latest by about the age of 30 years. It may be noted that the learning phase is called brahmacharya-ashram: a period of life in which self-control is learnt and practiced. Celibacy is the rule for this period, even though sexual union is possible. The Gruhsathashram –householder phase, can last up to the age of 60-70 years. Married life is the norm for the Hindu society, and satisfaction of all desires is encouraged. This ashrama is considered the mainstay of the society, sustaining the other three ashramas. We thus see that these two phases of life fit well into the life style of the modern world. The vanaprastha –leaving for forest - does not; in fact, though smrutis advised the dvija man and his wife (if willing) to leave the household and go to a forest for simple living after fulfilling his duties as a householder, this has been practiced only rarely since ca 400 CE. In the 21st century, high population density and small forest cover together make forest living on a large scale impossible. Since long, entering the Vanaprastha phase is the start of the process of detachment from worldly possessions. Handing over the responsibilities to the next generation is the first step, next is to give the new generation the freedom to take their own decisions on life and then to desist from interfering in their life. Also, emotional attachments to things (home, possessions of different kinds) and to persons (family, relatives, friends) is to be gradually reduced. It is not easy to bring about such changes in own life. Both men and women need to train themselves using considerable self-control to manage this process of detachment with a serenely happy state of mind. That is why a period of 15-20 years has been allotted to vanaprastha. The philosophies of Hinduism help in this phase and in the next phase of Sanyasa, total detachment in pursuit of moksha–liberation. Each Hindu man and woman in this last stage of life starting around 80-90 years of age is expected to realize that he/she is not the body but is an imperishable atma preparing to go over to another body soon. He/she owns it to the true self –the 'seer' or the atma - to continue to live with enthusiasm doing good karma till death claims the body. This would either lead to moksha after this death, or bring the atma nearer to moksha in the next birth.

Many Hindus continue to think in terms of these four phases of life in this modernized manner as we enter the 21st century. Whether one believes in atma, samsara and moksha or not, this phase wise way of living life parallels the natural processes where humans loose interest and faculties as they age.

Hinduism recommends that "It is better for you to abandon desires before the desires abandon you." This modernized thinking about the varna, ashrama and purushartha needs to spread wide through education in schools. This way of living life would possibly help to reduce self-centeredness and consumerism. Hopefully, the incidence of mental disorders would also be much less. This three dimensional social system is in fact quite secular, since the path to God is for a person to choose. Persons from other religions can choose their God and their own way of salvation. The non-believers can choose to not want anything like liberation, and be happy with the mental peace brought by this way of looking at life.

Manava Smruti

The constitution of India (1950) allowed each religion to have its own civil laws.[#] The criminal laws were taken out of the purview of all religions and made uniform throughout India. The social reforms made within Hinduism from 1810 till 1947 were consolidated legally via the Hindu Code Bills of 1956-1960. Civil laws decided the minimum age of marriage, ensured equal rights in ancestral estate to male and female children, prevented a man from having more than one (living) wife, allowed divorces and remarriages, permitted widow marriages etc. In effect, a completely new and truly ethical

---

[#] An attempt made in 1970s to bring in a uniform civil code for the entire nation proved unsuccessful, mainly because of opposition by the Muslims. An All India Muslim Personal Law Board was established in 1972 to ensure that the sharia laws remain applicable to Indian Muslims. If Hindus were to have insisted on the sanctity of Manusmruti and wanted to stick to it, the situation would have been similar. Fortunately, many Hindus with great moral courage went against the general sentiments of the Hindu society and fought for social justice to all men and women.

smruti has come into effect since 1960. This humane, fair and just smruti is indeed worthy of being termed Manava-smruti –a code for humans. The contradiction between the philosophy of Hinduism, where all atmas are part of the same parmatma, and its discriminating practices have been eliminated in principle. Several other aspects of behavior laid down by the smrutis on the prohibitions and the atonement for doing the prohibited etc. have also been abandoned. Religious rituals not meaningful in the industrialized world have been eliminated or kept voluntary. Ideas of impurity have been abandoned while keeping the good hygiene related practices. The situation has become so simplified, that a compilation of new smruti is no more necessary.

In practice, however, the behavioral change towards equality and liberty has been the greatest among the diaspora of Hindus outside India, around 90% as a good guess. The degree of improvement is similarly high in the big cities of India, somewhat less in the towns, and only around 60% in the villages. Behavioral changes in the other areas - taboos, ideas on impurity and belief in superstitions - have also permeated similarly in the different strata of Hindu society. Spread of education with a minimum of 10 years of schooling for all, and change of 2-3 generations will hopefully bring the entire Hindu society to the right level: equality and liberty would rule and the other demerits would also disappear to a large extent. We, of course, realize that ideals are never truly reached hundred percent.

CHAPTER 7
Dharma: Hinduism in Practice

The paths of Karmayoga and Dnyanayoga need no image or idol of an anthropomorphic God, and temples with idols installed in them. Their pursuits are mostly as individuals or in gatherings in halls or parks to listen to discourses. The large majority follows the path of Bhaktiyoga, where the saguna brahman manifests itself in many Gods. While no changes were necessary in the philosophies of Hinduism or in the paths of Karma and Dnyana, one major change was needed in the path of Bhakti –namely, elimination of superstitious beliefs. Most of these beliefs had no founding in scriptures –shrutis, smrutis, and puaranas. Examples are: the Goddess of smallpox, when angry, causes smallpox; rituals can ensure birth of a male child; bad influence of a variety of ghosts can be eliminated by specific rituals or by taking God's name; where a lizard falls on a person decides the kind of bad effect. Advances in science, spread of science education, large scale counseling in the context of inocculation against smallpox, polio etc. and perseverant efforts of organizations devoted to elimination of superstitions have together resulted in a large population of Hindus abandoning such superstitions. However, human race is gullible and complete eradication of superstitions does not appear to be feasible anywhere in the world.

The current practice of Hinduism is given under different headings to make them easy to understand. Two important points need to be noted: the topics covered under different headings would have some overlap; and the listing of items is only illustrative. An exhaustive listing is not feasible, given the great and diverse spread of Hindu life style. Fortunately, such listing is not necessary to understand the way in which Hinduism is practiced in the 21st century.

Gods of Hinduism: *deva-devi*

The triumvirate of Gods, Brahma-Vishnu-Mahesh, are the creator, the maintainer and the destroyer of the universe. Vishnu has many avataras –incarnations (appearance in this world in human form) –and the two most revered avataras are Rama and Krishna. Each God (and Goddess) has many names, usually adjectives and nouns referring to some aspect of benevolence of the particular God. Vishnu has more than thousand names. (Interestingly, most of the names of Hindu men and women are the names of Gods and Goddesses.) Mahesh is commonly known as Shiva and his consort Parvati or Durga is a revered Goddess. Rama's devotee, monkey–man Hanuman, also known as Maruti, is another revered God. So is Ganesha, son of Shiva-Parvati, who is God to be addressed first in any invocation or in any religious ceremony, because he is the remover of obstacles. Rama's wife Sita (fidelity), Vishnu's wife Laxmi (wealth), Ganesha's wife Saraswati (learning) is each a Goddess. Dattatreya, a three headed god, represents the trimurti –triumvirate –Brahma-Vishnu – Mahesh. Each god has an animal or a bird as his/her vehicle, and these animals also are revered. Since brahman occupies everything in the universe, everything and every being has a divine aspect and deserves reverence in Hinduism. The ancestors are revered and so also inanimate objects. The earth

-Prithvi – is a Goddess that sustains us and so deserves to be revered. Some rivers and some trees are sacred in the same way. The cow is a sacred animal: God Dattatreya is accompanied by a cow and four dogs, representing the four Vedas.

This godliness and reverence is seen in many expressions in common use in Bharat –India –since time immemorial: "Be one for whom a guest is God; Be one for whom Mother is God; Be one for whom Father is God." "Guru –teacher –is Brahma, is Vishnu, is Maheshwar, is manifested Parabrahman: bow to this shri – holy – Guru" Common greeting 'Namaste' means 'the divinity in me bows to the divinity in you'. It is common to use the names of Gods as greeting when people meet: 'Rama Rama, Jai (victory to)Shri Krishna, Jai Gurudev (teacher-god) Datta' are some examples.

Every family, each village, each sub-caste and caste have their own God or Goddess. Many a saints of the past, as recent as in the 20th century, are revered as Gods. Consequently, there exist innumerable Gods in Hinduism. Hindus in different states of India, each with its own language since over 1000 years, happen to give more importance to a certain deity as common tradition. To illustrate: Parvati is worshipped as Kali in Bengal, as Amba in Gujarat, and as Bhavani in Maharashtra. Shiva, also Datta, is more commonly worshipped in the four South Indian states Karnataka, Tamilnadu, Andhra Pradesh and Kerala. Krishna and Rama are revered all over India, but more so in the Northern states. A Hindu person may choose any one or more gods to worship and this happens without any sense of conflict between the different Gods. In fact, followers of each God or Goddess tend to give their particular deity the highest place in the hierarchy of Gods, equating him or her with the ultimate brahman.

Temples-*mandira*

God is literally omnipresent in Hinduism: each household has a place, a mini-temple, for its God(s) as idol(s) and/or as picture(s). All in the family, including the children, worship at this mini-temple (known as the 'house of god') two times a day; early morning after bath but before breakfast, and at dusk time when lamps are lighted, before meals. Prayers are said at the time of getting up, at meals, and at the time of going to sleep. Each of these is voluntary, to be done solely on the basis of what a person feels like doing. Most families establish a simple routine for children, who recite prayers at least once a day. Worship – pooja -consists of offering haldi-kumkum (yellow turmeric powder and a red powder made from it), and flowers, lighting a ghee (clarified butter) lamp, and singing hymns – aarati - while ringing a bell and circumambulating the lamp placed in a circular plate. Specific food items are then offered to the God and then distributed to all present at the worship as prasaad –blessing - from the God. Such worship takes place mostly in the mornings or in the evenings at dusk. Many versions of worship and prayer are available even within an extended family, and certainly within each (linguistic) state of India, and across different states. Here again, Hinduism proves to be the most democratic religion; each Hindu person is free to choose his/her own way of worshipping God.

Temples outside homes come in all sizes, from one metre square to huge complexes spread over several hectares. Small temples, with space only for the idol of a God, can be found along the sides of roads. Some person, usually a male, takes care of the temple and ensures that daily worship takes place. Some of those who pass by such temples will bow to the God and keep some coins as an offering to the God. This becomes the income of the person looking after the temple. The formal larger temples consist of a main hall -mandap, the sanctum – garbhagruha - where God's idol is established and, a rectangular or circular passage around the sanctorum for devotees to circumambulate around the deity in a clock wise manner–pradakshina. The temple has shape for the top structure and for the entrance to the temple area. The construction of temple building was standardized around 3000 BCE or even earlier and is followed for Hindu temples built anywhere in the world. Here also, several styles exist, and the temples of the North and the South are distinctively different. Only the priests, who are married men with family, are normally allowed in the sanctum. The priests perform pooja – worship – whereby the format is identical to the worship done at homes, but is more elaborate and rigorous. Priesthood was the exclusive privilege of Brahmin men till about the last quarter of the 20th century, but is now open to men from other varna/caste and also to women. The would-be priest needs to undergo appropriate training for priesthood. This training consists of studying Sanskrit and familiarizing with the general concepts of Hinduism and learning the details of many different kinds of worship and ceremonies like upanayana, marriage and after death, which are all in Sanskrit. On many occasions, it is now customary to explain the essence of Sanskrit texts in the language of the host and his guests. Even in the 21st century, Brahmin men are preferred as priests by most Hindus.

Devotional Songs: bhajana-satsanga

Small groups of men and women gather weekly or monthly by rotation at homes to sing bhajanas -devotional songs and to listen to discourses given by one from the group. This is termed as satsanga -company of the good (people who love God).

Fasts and Pledges: Upavaas and vrata

As aids to instill self-control, fasts -upavasa, being near (god) - are a common practice. The fasting day is from sunrise to sunrise. Fasts can mean eating restricted food items, not eating any food or even not drinking any fluid. Fasts are performed on specific day of week or month; and people opt out of non-vegetarian food during the four months of monsoon rains. Giving up on a food item one likes or deciding to recite selected verses daily for a specified period is vrata - a way of expressing gratitude to God.

Holy Places-(punyasthala) tirtha

Hindus worshipping different gods were and are kept united in religion on this vast subcontinent by inducing them to visit holy places spread all over in India. From ancient times, eight cities have been considered holy: Ayodhya (Rama), Mathura (Krishna), Maya-Haridwar (Shiva and Vishnu), Kashi (Shiva), Kanchi (Vishnu and Shiva), Avantika-Ujjain (Shiva), Puri-Jagannath (Krishna), Dwaravati-Dwarka (Krishna). Hundreds of more such holy places are popular destinations: these are famous either for the temples of specific god(s), or because these are places associated with saints and holy men/women.

Pilgrimage-*tirtha-yaaatraa*

Popular pilgrimages to holy places –yatras - across the country that encourage Hindus from different parts of India to come together are: char dhaam –four homes: Badrinath-Kedarnath(Shiva),Gangotri-Jamnotri (origins of Ganga and Yamuna rivers) in the Western Himalayas; twelve Jyotirlingas (Shiva) in NEWS of Bharat, Somnath, Ujjain, Tryambak, Rameshwar, SriShail, Banaras among them ; eight Vinayakas (Ganesha) in Maharashtra, Nath Dwara (Krishna) in Rajasthan, Tirupati (Vishnu) in Tamilnadu and Guruvayur (Krishna) in Kerala. Mansarovar (Manas lake) now in Tibet, Amarnath (Shiva) and Vaishnodevi (Shakti - Durga) in Jammu and Kashmir, Deoghar (Shiva) in Jharkhand. Pandharpur (Vitthal –Vishnu) in Maharashtra, and Dakor (Krishna) in Gujarat have traditions of over hundreds of years whereby men and women of all castes walk together for several days over 100 km to reach the temples of their deity at specific times of the year. Kumbha Mela –'earthen pot' gathering -takes place every four years at Haridwar, Nasik, Ujjain and Prayag (Allahabad). The Mahakumbha Mela at Prayag every 12 years is at the Triveni Sangam-confluence of three holy rivers, Ganges, Jamuna and Saraswati (now extinct); the attendance at this Maha-kumbha is in millions.

Festivals: *utsav*

Hindu festivals are celebrations of good over evil, commemoration of births and of great occasions in the lives of Gods, and worship of different Gods for specific purposes. The festivals were planned to fall on specific days of the Hindu calendar (though five different calendars are in use - three lunar and two solar - the days happen to be the same all over

India) at times convenient for the agriculture based civilization. The importance given to a festival in a state depends on long standing cultural traditions and the prominent deity in the state.

Some major festivals are: New year (3 lunar, 2 solar); Makar Sankranti (14th January), the Sun-God enters the northern hemisphere; Vasanta-panchami, for Goddess Saraswati of learning; Maha-Shivaratri, a night to worship Shiva; Holi, the festival of colours (Lord Vishnu) ; Rama-navami (birth of God Rama), Raksha-bandhan, brothers protecting sisters; Hanuman-jayanti, birth of Lord Hanuman; Guru-pournima, venerating the guru; Janma-ashtami, birth of Lord Krishna; Ganesh-utsav, 10 days of worshipping Lord Ganesha; Nava-ratri, a nine day festival to worship Goddess Durga ending with Vjaya-dashmi (Dusehra); Deepavali, 3/5/7 days festival of light. Nav-ratri is celebrated in Gujarat with men and women dancing together to worship Amba, while in Bengal it is Durga-puja festival. Holi is a joyous festival for men and women together mainly in the North. Ratha-yatra at Puri in the east is a pilgrimage cum festival of chariot carrying Jagan-natha –Vishnu, the Lord of the World. The year is so full of Hindu festivals and special days of worship, that giving holidays on each of them would mean working for about only half of the year!

Sects: *sampradaaya*

Sampradaya is a religious tradition passed on by a succession of masters and disciples who take their specific preaching to the lay population for improving their spiritual cum religious life. Many Hindu sampradayas flourish in India and most have reached also the Hindu diaspora. Viashnav – Lord Vishnu's – sampradyas are: Ramanandi, Gaudiya, Pushtimarga (Vallabhi), and Swaminarayan. Shaiva –Lord Shiva's – sampradayas are Nath and Dash-naami; while Vedanta sampradayas/maths are at Govardhan, Sringeri, Dwarakà and Jyotirmath, each led by a designated Shankaracharya. The Arya Samaj, started in late 19th century, is also a major sampradaya. Each smapradaya (and its sub-sects) has thousands of followers, some have millions of followers.

Although these sampradayas do not observe caste distinctions, their followers have mostly been from the three dvija varnas. Consequently, since the 13th century, sampradayas have been started by saints from the shoodra castes and they have also flourished: for example, Ghasidasa (ca 1800) from the cobbler's community who cited Vedas in his support. The Sant-naama panth that he started then had over 20,000 followers. The other sampradayas, known as better as panthas (paths) were those of Kabir and Sai Baba of Shirdi: these saints were and are revered by both Hindus and Muslims.

Saints: *sant*

A Hindu sant - saint - is a holy person, an ascetic who has surrendered completely to God, to the will of God and who lives a life of total devotion. The word sant means a seeker of truth –sat. Bharat has a long tradition of saints over more than 2000 years. People, recognizing the way of living and the deeds of a person, begin to consider him or her as a saintly person, and then they start following his/her teachings. Saints appeared in all states. They came from all four varnas (and castes), including the lowest of shoodra castes. Only a few of the saints from about 500 CE to 1700 CE are mentioned below. Most of these were saint-poets and their poems are recited or sung all over India in the 21st century also.

Dnyaneshwar(Brahmin), Eknath(Brahmin), Namdev(tailer), Tukaram(grocer), Ramdas(Brahmin), Chokha Mela (sweeper),Sawanta Mali (gardner) and Gora Kumbhar (potter) are some men saint-poets from Maharashtra. Their castes are shown in brackets to demonstrate that Hindu saints in all provinces were from different castes. Women saints (ma or bai) of Maharashtra are Muktabai, and Janabai. Some other well-known saint poets are: Narsi Mehta and Jalaram Bapa from Gujarat; Tulsidas, Krishna Balaram Swami, and Neem Karoli Baba from Uttar Pradesh; Kabir from Punjab; Ghasidas from Chhattisgarh, Darya Saheb from Bihar; Meerabai, Dadu Dayal from Rajastahan; Chaitanya Mahaprabhu, Ramakrishna Paramahansa, Swami Vivekananda and Sri Aurobindo from Bengal; Alwars (16 vaishanva saints) and Nayanmaars (63 shaiva saints), Swami Sivananda of Tamilnadu; Thyagaraja, Ramana Mahrshi, Satya Sai Baba from Andhra Pradesh; Vadiraja Tirtha, Jayatirtha, Basavanna and Akkamahadevi from Karnataka; Ma Amritapuri from Kerala: Anandamayi Ma from the East.

Teacher: *guru*

Hindu gurus are of two general kinds: those who give discourses on aspects of religion, either philosophical or in the form of stories with moral teachings from the epics or the puranas; and those who also teach specific techniques for daily follow up by the pupils from lay society, mostly householders.

The proponents of the Theosophical Society, Acharya Rajaneesh (later known as Osho), J. Krishnamurthy are among the philosophy gurus. Morari Bapu, Pandurangshastri Athawale and others base their discourses on puranas and epics. Swami Chinmayanada, Swami Bodhanada are some examples of gurus giving discourses based on Vedas, Upanishadas and Bhagavad-Geeta.

The gurus propagating methodologies for self-elevation and mental peace that have originated from Hinduism are: BKS Aiyangar for yogasanas, Mahesh Yogi for Transcendental Meditation, Paramahansa Yogananda for Kriya Yoga, Swami Parthasarathy for Vedanta, Rishi Prabhakar for Siddhi Samadhi Yoga, Balyogishwar or Maharaji for Breath Awareness, Sri Sri Ravishankar for Art of Living, Sadhguru for Isha Yoga. All of these and many more, have gone also outside India, in all continents of the world. These gurus have rightly dissociated these methods from the 'worship of Hindu Gods' and hence from Hinduism as a 'religion' (as the word religion is generally understood world over, but is different from the concept of dharma). Each of these techniques is completely secular in the sense that a person from any religion can follow them for own benefit while remaining firmly within own religion. The philosophical basis of the soul of a person being the same as the great soul –atma as paramatma –is often used explicitly, while the idea of samsara –the cycle of birth and rebirth - is not quite necessary. The idea that each living being is a manifestation of the indescribable brahman, since the principle of consciousness exists in all beings, is universally acceptable. Those who follow the method advocated by any of such gurus can succeed in getting the desired results. Since this success is experientially verifiable by each practitioner, the spread of these methods has been very wide all over the world. We note that the deliberate dissociation of any of these methodologies from worship of gods of Hinduism has helped considerably in getting world-wide acceptance of these gurus and their methods of self-help.

Missions: *matha*

Religion related missions can be defined as organizations established to spread a particular doctrine. Hinduism had such a tradition of establishing a matha and creating a cadre of disciples cum preachers who would propagate their particular path of Hinduism. A matha is presided over by a Swami, who is chosen from among the many disciple Swamis (ascetics). The earliest mathas were the four established by Adi Shankara in ca 820 CE at four places mentioned earlier. The natha sampradaya had established many mathas for Shiva worship. Sant Ramdas in the 17th century established 12 mathas for spreading the worship of Lord Rama. Swami Vivekananda established the Ramkrishna Matha and Mission in early 20th century, Swami Chinmayananda established the Chinmaya Mission in the middle of the 20th century. Arya Samaj and ISKCON –International Society for Krishna CONscoiusnes - are also missions.

Retreats: *ashrama*

These are hermitages or residential retreats where the seekers can go and stay for a few days and live life as prescribed by the guru. Many ashramas are available in India and in the West; thses are expected to be run on a no-profit basis. The daily routine consists of getting up early morning before dawn, engaging in some form of asana-pranayaam-meditation after ablutions, listening to discourses and singing bhajana – religious songs etc. Questioning and seeking answers is welcome during the discourses, but raising an argument on any idea is not expected. Such retreats are usually of 5 to 15 days duration. Where the hermitage permits a person to come and be by himself/herself in quietude, the duration can be even up to six months. People generally go for stays at ashramas after retirement: in their Vanaprastha or Sanyasa phase of life. Some ashramas combine natural health improvement through controlled diet and exercise: such hermitages are used by also by people in the Gruhasthashrama (who are working for their livelihood) for improving mental and physical health. Such programs are of 14 - 21 days.

A Hindu is free to choose to practice any one or more forms described in this chapter; nothing is mandatory.

Many non-Hindus attend discourses by gurus, practice the yoga related techniques and reside in hermitages to improve health/fitness, to gain knowledge and to experience mental peace of high order.

CHAPTER 8
Dharma: New World Hinduism

This brief review of the beginning of Hinduism and its adapting to changing environment over seven millennia has shown that Hinduism is now rejuvenated to flourish in the centuries to come. However, some peripheral but important aspects have remained untouched. So, this final chapter deals with the stance of Hinduism towards science, other religions and ecology; and also with its vision for the future.

Hinduism and Science

Unlike in Europe, where the discoveries in science were perceived as going against the Christian scripture (Bible), Hinduism had no conflict with any scientific discovery. Heliocentricity, i.e. the earth's movement around the sun, was known in India in the 5th century, but its originator, Aryabhata, faced no boycott or punishment of any kind. The Hindus had stipulated the existence of two planets, Rahu and Ketu, who cause eclipse of the sun and the moon. When modern science showed that eclipses are shadow effects, it has been so accepted unconditionally. (Hindu astrology continues to live merrily with these two fictitious planets!) Darwin's theory of evolution did not disturb since Hindus had believed in the ten incarnations of Lord Vishnu, whereby the first is a fish, a waterborne animal. The second is an amphibian, the turtle. The third is a land based animal, boar, and the next is half-human half-animal, nara-simha. This story of incarnations, unique to Hinduism, runs parallel to the story of evolution as established by the scientific method. Since Hindus revere a monkey God, the fact that our ancestors were monkeys does not disturb them. Additionally, Hinduism states that a soul goes through 8.4 million birth cycles before getting the highest of body form, namely, the human form; this order of magnitude tallies with Darwinian stages of evolution and diversity. Even the idea of the universe coming out of nothing and going to nothing in a cycle of 4.32 billion years seems similar to what the modern physicists postulate. However, we need to note that these and such other observations happen to be convenient coincidences which have helped Hinduism and Hindus to accept the results of the scientific method.

In principle, Hinduism sees no conflict between science and dharma (religion) because dharma deals with the subject (I – ahankara or the ego-principle, atma -soul etc.) while science looks at the object (physical matter, including human body and mind). Like philosophy, Hinduism seeks answers to questions like 'the purpose of life' and the 'goal of life'. Science does not seek any *purpose* in its quest; it seeks answers to the questions of 'why' in the sense of 'how' natural phenomena take place. When it comes to establishing 'truth' about the cause and effect in natural phenomena, the scientific method has proved itself to be the best available tool for mankind. This realization had dawned on the Hindu reformers of the 19th and 20th century: even staunch Hindus publicly said, 'Revere the Vedas and Puranas, but use the conclusions of science to base our societal system on principles of equality of all men and women.'

Hinduism and Other Religions

One of the core concepts in Hinduism is that there are many paths to the same goal –God or salvation of some kind. Therefore, neither at the early stage of the sanatana dharma nor after it turned into Hinduism did this religion try to spread by asking other people to become Hindus nor did it try to suppress any other religion. The spirit was to let each community choose its way of life and path to after-life and to God.

The sanatana dharma –eternal religion – has dealt with other religions since 5000 BCE. When the Aryans came into Bharatvarsha, they found an indigenous religion based on devotion to Shiva-linga (linga means phallus, sign, gender etc.). The prolonged interaction between them resulted in each adopting some ways of the other. The result was Hinduism as we know it today. Another impact came in around 700 BCE. If some wished to follow the tenets of Tirthankar Mahavira and become Jains, that was accepted. If some others wished to follow Gautama Buddha and call themselves Buddhists, that was also accepted. These followers of other paths were neither persecuted nor boycotted. The rulers who adopted Buddhism as their 'religion' did not persecute the followers of the sanatana dharma nor stopped helping them from their treasuries. All three religions received support from the rulers. Jainism flourished, but the percentage of Jains remained small in the population. Though Buddhism attracted men and women from all castes to become ascetics, the lay public was apparently unaffected. Many ideas and methods of Jainism and Buddhism were from sanatana dharma and so the conflict was minimal. Hinduism literally absorbed Buddhism by considering Buddha as the 9th incarnation of Lord Vishnu.

Later, the efforts of Adi Shankaracharya succeeded in reducing the influence of Buddhism on the householders.

Islam and Hinduism have had adversarial relations mainly because Islam is staunch in the belief that only that religion is the right one for humanity. Moreover, most Muslim rulers considered spreading of Islam as their sacred duty. Attempts of Hindus to reconcile with Islam - turned out to be one-sided. Mahatma Gandhi tried to develop brotherhood between Muslims and Hindus. His bhajan –hymn –mentioned that Ishwar and Allah are names of the same God. Most Hindus feel this way, but no Muslim would dare admit to such a blasphemy; Quran states that Allah is the only God, and enjoins its believers to destroy idols. The history of forced conversions of 'kafirs', of extra taxes on Hindus from time to time as per Sharia/Quran, of wanton destruction of Hindu temples, and of atrocities of the Muslim rulers (though not in the name of Islam) on Hindus (especially on the women) have resulted in a strong mistrust of Muslims among Hindus in general. The creation of Pakistan on the basis of a two nation theory where religion was equated with nationality, the bloodshed during partition of British India (1947-48), and the atrocities committed by the Wahhabi Sunni/Taliban fractions of Islam in the name of jihad (1980 onward) have further confounded the relationship. Hindu-Muslim riots have erupted in different parts of India since 1900 or so, and the latest was in 2013. Such riots are more socio-political than religious. The non-Muslims other than Christians and Jews (both termed as followers of 'book religions' in Quran) are given only two options in Quran: the kafirs must either be converted to Islam or be killed. Modern Islam does not want to follow such tenets; but no religious leader has openly said that this concept is not meaningful in the world of multiple religions. Fortunately, a large majority of Indian Muslims have consciously avoided such unethical dicta of Islam and have stayed away from unethical tenets of Sharia laws also. Most Indian Muslims, as patriotic as their counterparts from other religions of India, know that Hinduism per se, welcomes them to follow their religion peacefully. They live together in a feeling of mutual acceptance of faiths in the secular democracy that India has adopted.

Hindus encouraged Sikhism in its early years: it was common to find Hindu families encouraging one son to become Sikh. The tenets of Sikhism are similar to some of Hinduism. Their sacred book –Guru Granth Sahib –contains verses/poems to be sung in different ragas (melodies). Many of the verses composed by Hindu and Muslim saints are included in this sacred book. The relationship between Hindus and Sikhs has been quite cordial, of mutual respect for religious traditions. However, there was one period of major exception: 1970 to 1990. During this period, some Sikhs, mainly from outside India, had demanded a separate nation for the Sikhs. The Khalsa brigades (termed terrorists by all Indians) selectively executed Hindu civilians. The main shrine of Sikhs, the Golden Temple at Amritsar, was occupied by armed terrorists and the Indian army was asked to remove them, which lead to the assassination of the Prime Minister Indira Gandhi by her Sikh bodyguard. The riots that resulted caused tremendous loss of property and life for the Sikhs all over India. But this damage to the relationship has been repaired thereafter. We again note that this disturbance was political.

Christianity and Hinduism had adversarial relations during the periods when some Christian missionaries tried to ridicule

Hinduism in their efforts to gain converts. Normally, however, the relationship has been cordial over 2000 years. In the 20th century, several Christian sects in the West have accepted that other paths than Christianity can also lead to the grace of god. This was also stated officially by the Pope in 1994. This permits Christianity to tolerate Hinduism. However, this has not stopped Christians wanting to convert Indians – Hindus, not Muslims nor Sikhs –to Christianity. They concentrate efforts on tribals and dalits: in South India – mainly in Tamilnadu – also on the so-called 'Dravidians'. Secularly titled institutions, funded by Christian groups, that study history of Indian languages and culture make false claims about Christianity having helped shape the religious concepts and cultural expressions in Tamilnadu. These efforts divide Indians into adversary groups and are likely to lead to undesired confrontations.

In 1956, Dr. B. R. Ambedkar asked *dalits* (untouchables) to convert and become Buddhists (0.8% in India: 2011 census). Most Indian Jews migrated to Israel after 1950s. The Parsees, who do not marry outsiders or admit others into Zoroastrianism, are dwindling in number. The Baha'is are growing gradually. None of these religions have any conflict with Hinduism.

The constitution of India permits each religion to propagate and to seek conversion, but neither by force nor by inducements. Only the conversions based on religious preference are welcome.

The strongest test of social relationship between persons from different religions or races with each other is the attitude toward inter-religion or inter-racial marriages. As we enter the 21st century, Hindu girls and boys choosing spouses from another religion are no more uncommon. Such marriages are not liked, but are tolerated in India, and accepted within the Hindu diaspora spread world-wide. If both spouses agree to not change their religion, then marriages get better accepted. The problem comes only when either the boy's or the girl's family insists on conversion before marriage. This happens mostly where one of the spouses is Muslim; conversion to Islam is often insisted upon. Fortunately, such insistence is becoming less frequent. Earlier, Hindu priests were reluctant to convert even willing bride or groom to Hinduism; only the Arya Samaj welcomed such conversions. Now, the situation has improved: conversion to Hinduism is welcome. Many couples get married legally in a civil marriage registered in a court of law. Some marry twice: once by Hindu ceremony and once by Christian ceremony, for example. The decision on the religion to be followed by the children of such mixed marriages is taken by parents; a correct picture of what happens in such cases as a general trend will emerge after a few more generations.

Hinduism and Ecology

The need for conserving nature is a recent need of mankind, arising out of the global warming caused by industrialization. It has taken over 200 years of 'progress' for us to realize that the pollution caused by many operations like burning of fossil fuels is adversely affecting the natural balance of different life cycles and atmospheric cycles. All the religions of the world had started before industrialization began and would have, therefore, felt no need to consider nature conservation as a duty of humans. Consequently, no religion addresses nature conservation directly

In Judaism, Christianity and Islam, God has created the world for the humans; exploiting nature for the benefit of mankind is therefore considered normal. In Hinduism, the concept of brahman being present in all sentient and insentient beings makes a different statement. Mountains, rivers, trees, animals all receive reverence; many prayers are for the wellbeing of all living organisms. As a result of this reverence, the movements for reducing pollution of atmosphere and for conserving the biodiversity of the world receive popular support more easily in India.

Hinduism: Future Vision

Till about the 19th century, one had to be born in a Hindu family to be a Hindu, and Hindus were almost exclusively in India (and Nepal). Hinduism and India were inseparables. As we enter the 21st century, any person in the world can become a Hindu, and Hindus are spread world over. Hindus have adopted the nationality of the country to which they have immigrated. Nationals of countries other than India (and Nepal) have converted to Hinduism. So, Hindus need not be Indian nationals: being Hindu is a religious statement, not a statement of nationality, as is the case with Christians and Muslims. Indian citizens follow more than seven different religions; the Indian-ness of other than Hindus or their patriotism toward their nation – India –is as strong as that of Hindus. Hinduism as a religion needs to be freed from Hindu nationalism, which is a political statement.

The three distinct paths to liberation, the egalitarian varna-ashram-purushartha system based on equality and liberty, and the methodologies like yoga-pranayam-meditation are such that these can be followed universally by people of all religions. The concepts and prescribed behaviors of the four ashramas and the four purusharthas are worth adopting, voluntarily and without any need for changing religious affiliation, to achieve a balanced and happy life. The advantages offered by these practices for good mental and physical health are now well established and are being availed by millions of people. These concepts need to spread even wider, especially as societies become affluent and loose bearing in excessive self-centered-ness and addictive consumerism.

Lastly, the three paths of reaching liberation (or nearness to God, or salvation or serenity) provide a neat schema for all religions of the world to respect every other religion and to live peacefully with persons following any other religion.

SELECTED BIBLIOGRAPHY

1. The Arctic Home in the Vedas, B.G. Tilak, Messers Tilak Brothers, 1903
2. The wonder that was India, A.L. Basham, Collins London 1954
3. Advanced History of India, P.T. Srinivasa Iyengar,
4. Hinduism R.C. Zaechner, Oxford University Press, 1968
5. Insights into Hinduism, R.N. Dandekar, Ajanta Publications (India), Delhi, 1979
6. How to become a Hindu, S. Sivaya Subramaniyaswami, Himalaya Academy, 1989
7. India through the Ages, Jadunath Sarkar, 1992
8. Meeting God: Elements of Hindu Devotion, Stephen Huyler, Yale Univ. Press, 1999
9. Social and Religious Reforms: The Hindus of British India, Ed. Amiya P. Sen, Oxford University Press, 2003
10. A Vision for Hinduism: Beyond Hindu Nationalism, Jeffery D. Long, IB Tauris, 2007
11. Breaking India: Western Interventions in Dravidian and Dalit Faultlines, Rajiv Malhotra and Aravindan. Neelakandan, Amaryllis, 2011
12. Being Different: An Indian Challenge to Western Universalism, Rajiv Malhotra, Harper Collins India, 2011